Cheryl A. Hunter

Myths and Archetypes in "The Lord of the Rings" and "Harry Potter"

Cheryl A. Hunter

Myths and Archetypes in "The Lord of the Rings" and "Harry Potter"

Mythological Heroes and the Hero and Journey Archetype

LAP LAMBERT Academic Publishing

Impressum/Imprint (nur für Deutschland/ only for Germany)
Bibliografische Information der Deutschen Nationalbibliothek: Die Deutsche Nationalbibliothek
verzeichnet diese Publikation in der Deutschen Nationalbibliografie; detaillierte bibliografische
Daten sind im Internet über http://dnb.d-nb.de abrufbar.
Alle in diesem Buch genannten Marken und Produktnamen unterliegen warenzeichen-, marken-
oder patentrechtlichem Schutz bzw. sind Warenzeichen oder eingetragene Warenzeichen der
jeweiligen Inhaber. Die Wiedergabe von Marken, Produktnamen, Gebrauchsnamen,
Handelsnamen, Warenbezeichnungen u.s.w. in diesem Werk berechtigt auch ohne besondere
Kennzeichnung nicht zu der Annahme, dass solche Namen im Sinne der Warenzeichen- und
Markenschutzgesetzgebung als frei zu betrachten wären und daher von jedermann benutzt
werden dürften.

Coverbild: www.ingimage.com

Verlag: LAP LAMBERT Academic Publishing GmbH & Co. KG
Dudweiler Landstr. 99, 66123 Saarbrücken, Deutschland
Telefon +49 681 3720-310, Telefax +49 681 3720-3109
Email: info@lap-publishing.com

Herstellung in Deutschland:
Schaltungsdienst Lange o.H.G., Berlin
Books on Demand GmbH, Norderstedt
Reha GmbH, Saarbrücken
Amazon Distribution GmbH, Leipzig
ISBN: 978-3-8443-0074-1

Imprint (only for USA, GB)
Bibliographic information published by the Deutsche Nationalbibliothek: The Deutsche
Nationalbibliothek lists this publication in the Deutsche Nationalbibliografie; detailed
bibliographic data are available in the Internet at http://dnb.d-nb.de.
Any brand names and product names mentioned in this book are subject to trademark, brand
or patent protection and are trademarks or registered trademarks of their respective holders.
The use of brand names, product names, common names, trade names, product descriptions
etc. even without a particular marking in this works is in no way to be construed to mean that
such names may be regarded as unrestricted in respect of trademark and brand protection
legislation and could thus be used by anyone.

Cover image: www.ingimage.com

Publisher: LAP LAMBERT Academic Publishing GmbH & Co. KG
Dudweiler Landstr. 99, 66123 Saarbrücken, Germany
Phone +49 681 3720-310, Fax +49 681 3720-3109
Email: info@lap-publishing.com

Printed in the U.S.A.
Printed in the U.K. by (see last page)
ISBN: 978-3-8443-0074-1

DEDICATION

This book is dedicated to my daughter Audrey, my research assistant. Your love and enthusiasm for "The Lord of the Rings" and "Harry Potter" has been infectious. I cherish the many hours we spent discussing the books and the movies.

ACKNOWLEDGEMENTS

Thank you to my family and friends for your support through my many endeavors. Your love means a great deal to me.

Special thanks to my dad for helping not only with this project but for everything you have done for me throughout my life.

TABLE OF CONTENTS

CHAPTER I

MYTHOLOGY

Development of Mythology

Why are humans on earth? What role do the gods play in human life? These are some of the questions humans of all cultures have been asking for millennia. Mythology began as a way to answer questions about life, explain tradition, establish culture, and educate people. From the world's oldest stories to contemporary, young adult, high fantasy novels such as "The Lord of the Rings," and "Harry Potter", mythology is a relevant and indispensable component of literature. Its inclusion adds complexity to the stories, and through the use of literary devices, such as the archetypes of the hero and the journey, basic universal human truths and values upon which modern society is built are imparted to the reader.

Myths are essentially the stories of a culture. Myth is defined in A Handbook to Literature as "an anonymous story that presents supernatural episodes as a means of interpreting natural events" (Harmon 325). Mythology, a compilation of these myths, attempts "to explain creation, divinity, and religion; to probe the meaning of existence and death; to account for natural phenomena; and to chronicle the adventures of cultural heroes" (Harmon 326). All cultures have these stories.

Myths are of many and varied types, including hero myths, creation myths, love and marriage myths, and nature myths. Each type of myth encompasses timeless and universal themes, such as love, birth, marriage, death, greed, goodness, and coming of age. Joseph Campbell, author of several books on mythology and modern culture, taught that universal themes are as relevant to modern people as they were to ancient Greek and Roman people because myths "offer life models" for people to refer to when faced with difficult decisions and situations ("Power of Myth" 16). Since myths exhibit universal themes "they must in some way represent features of our general racial imagination, permanent features of the human spirit – or, as we say today, of the psyche" (Campbell "Myths" 26). The stories of mythology may be "among the oldest in the world…[and] their meaning has been transformed from generation to generation and from writer to writer" (Frye "Biblical and Classical Myths" 277). Although the particulars of the stories may vary, many of the stories are similar, and these deeper meaning and themes are the same even between cultures that have never had contact.

Myths provide a guide to life from which children can learn when faced with problems in their own lives. Children are impressionable and the rules of society must be taught to a child at an early age. Rituals that arise out of mythology can help teach a child about society and his or her role within that society. Therefore, "by absorbing the myths of his [or her] social group and participating in its rites, the youngster is structured to accord with his [or her] social as well as natural environment, and [he or she] is turned from an amorphous nature product, prematurely born, into a defined and competent member of some specific, efficiently functioning social order" (Campbell "Myths" 45). Myths have provided people with guidance for thousands of years and provide "perspective on what's happening to you" today (Campbell "Power of Myth" 2). Reading and understanding myths provide insight into "the inner problems, inner mysteries, inner thresholds of passage" of life, and children can draw on that knowledge to help them deal with situations in their own lives. (Campbell "Power of Myth" 2) Therefore, the value of mythology cannot be understated.

Mythology establishes a society's cultural identity by conveying knowledge, history and tradition, and by explaining an individual's roles within society. "Myth is the most ancient kind of story-telling" (Frye "Biblical and Classical Myths" 277) because myths have been around for thousands of years. When ancient people listened to the stories they believed that the events and people in the stories were actually part of their society's past. Today, we refer to these ancient stories as mythology, implying they are fantasy, but to ancient people these stories represented their history, were the basis of their religion, and were believed to be true.

Storytelling is a trait of human beings, and the oral tradition dates back to primitive cavemen. In Myths to Live By, Joseph Campbell states, "mythology is apparently coeval with mankind" (21) because when we consider "the psychological character of our species, the most evident distinguishing sign is man's organization of his life according primarily to mythic, and only secondarily economic aims and laws" (22). According to Campbell, human beings place the mythic above all, including economics, because, unlike animals, a human being is "aware that he, and all he cares for, will one day die" (22), and mythology helps ease the anxiety that humans experience as a result of this knowledge.

Recognition of mortality has led humans to question their existence on the Earth and their role in nature. Recognition of their own mortality has also led to humans' desire for and belief in an afterlife and the attempt to preserve a legacy by which they can be remembered by successive generations. Archeologists have uncovered evidence of Neanderthal Man's recognition of mortality and his desire to transcend death at burial sites. Buried with the body, archeologists found tools, sacrificed animals, and other necessary supplies for the afterlife, but whether Neanderthal Man practiced religion is uncertain. In her October 2002 article for the American Association for the Advancement of Science, Monica Amarelo states that at sites of habitation by Cro-Magnon Man "evidence emerged of the elaborate burial, with hints of ritual and belief in an afterlife" (1). The bodies of the dead were buried with valuable items, such as elaborate clothing and carved pendants that indicate an effort to adorn the dead. Amarelo further states, "in all human societies, the burial of the dead with grave adornments indicates a belief in an afterlife," suggesting that Cro-Magnon man recognized mortality and hoped for an afterlife. The burial practices of the Upper Paleolithic humans are also "in accordance with an afterlife, a continuation of earthly life" (Vialou 133) because of the layout of the bodies and the ornamentations buried with the bodies. Scholars believe these burial practices "were doubtless dictated by certain mythologies" (Vialou 133) indicating that mythology has been an integral part of life for humans for thousands of years.

According to many scholars, recognition of mortality is one of three distinguishing characteristics of human psychology that separates humans from animals. First, humans understand the meaning of death and they recognize that they will one day die. Second, humans understand that the social group to which they belong "was flourishing long before his [or her] own birth and will remain when he [or she] is gone" (Campbell, "Myths" 22). Humans realize that an individual's life is short in comparison to society's duration, and this triggers a desire to transcend life. The individual is compelled to adapt himself or herself to "the community into which he [or she] has been born, this being an order of life superordinated to his [or her] own; a superorganization into which he [or she] must allow himself [or herself] to be absorbed, and through participation in which he [or she] will come to know the life that transcends death" (Campbell, "Myths" 22). The inevitability of death and the endurance of society form the basis of rites and rituals that bind members of the society and create mythology. The third characteristic of human psychology relevant to mythology comes from the individual's recognition of the world and the desire to understand it. Mythology developed because of the need to explain the world. For example, nature and creation myths arose because of the necessity to explain the natural phenomena that were a source of anxiety for humans. These myths are the type of myths common to all cultures around the world.

The earliest myths taught people how to live communally, how to hunt, and how to survive. Basic hunting myths connected the hunter and the prey in a ritualistic ceremony. Many cave paintings from the Paleolithic Age are found in isolated and difficult to reach locations that suggest to many scholars that they have religious connotations. One theory is that "prehistoric hunters attributed magical properties to the images they painted and sculpted" (Gardner 8). The images were a form of "hunting magic that were made as part of a ritual" of hunting (Janson 42). Early men respected and revered the animals they hunted for food and clothing because of the danger involved in hunting. When hunting with a spear, or bow and arrow, the hunter must get very close to the prey, and myths and rituals prepare the hunter for that difficult and dangerous task.

The human desire to explain natural phenomena, life, society, and man's place in the universe shaped the mythology that has been passed down through the millennia. Early storytellers taught the young and old using oral myths, just as today books are used to instruct all ages of the population. Rituals develop from myths and together they form an instruction manual for life. Ancient myths and rituals "were designed to harmonize the mind and the body (Campbell, "Power of Myth" 87), and they are important because they provide guidance for every stage of human development from birth to death by telling "how others have made the passage" (Campbell, "Power of Myth" 87). Myths are the stories "we have told from the dawn of time, to explain the world around us, and to make sense of our place within it" (Randall 7). Myths bind people together in a community and explain how the community was created and has survived adversity.

Mythology in Children's Literature

One way for individuals to learn about the heritage and the culture from which they are descended is literature. Storytelling has been a part of human society for thousands of years as evidenced by the cave paintings in France that date back to 31,000 years ago.[i] The paintings convey history, philosophy, culture, and tradition to present generations of humans, and this is important because their education ensures the continuation of the stories into the future. Through the literature they read at home and at school, children learn lessons from mythology that they can draw on when faced with a problem or difficulty. Myths are stories about life, and when a child reads these stories he or she is left "fantasizing whether and how to apply to himself [or herself] what the story reveals about life and human nature" (Bettelheim "Enchantment" 45). The child can then apply the lessons from the story to his or her everyday life.

Mythology and children's literature often teach lessons about the stages of life, such as coming of age, which is the process of moving from childhood to adulthood. Children's literature that incorporates myths provides children with life models and establishes a connection with the people from whom the child is culturally descended. In most cultures and religions there are rituals associated with events, such as coming of age, that help a child recognize the transition to adulthood and publicly mark the occasion.

Good and evil are two of the universal values upon which every society is based, and the theme of good and evil is prevalent in mythology and in modern literature, especially in modern children's literature. Mythology has once again become popular in society because of the success of movies such as "The Lord of the Rings" and the "Harry Potter" series, which have become cultural icons and have attained cult status. The authors of the books on which the movies are based have intentionally incorporated elements of classical mythology into the stories, elements that many people unfamiliar with ancient culture miss.

There are many books on mythology available to readers of all ages. Edith Hamilton's Mythology is a collection of Greco-Roman myths for adults and young adults. The myths are arranged by categories and Hamilton devotes considerable space to the heroes of mythology. The Odyssey adapted by Robin Lister is a richly illustrated account of Odysseus' journey back from Troy for young adult readers. In addition, D'Aulaire's Book of Greek Myths is a beautifully illustrated book of classic Greek myths for children. [ii]

Joseph Campbell, a noted scholar and writer, saw the importance of mythology in modern culture and has written many books that explore the relevance of myth to modern society. He discusses the importance of mythology to children, and often references "Star Wars", which was the latest hero and journey story of the time. The Hero with a Thousand Faces details the hero archetype for the reader and offers examples of its inclusion in literature by using a variety of ancient and modern texts. He makes extensive use of Biblical and other religious stories when analyzing and illustrating the hero archetype. Myths to Live By is based on Campbell's lectures on mythology and the questions he received after those lectures. The result of Campbell's books, his popularity, and his insights led to a PBS interview with journalist Bill Moyers. The Power of Myth is a transcript of that interview. In the book, Campbell is asked about the symbols of mythology that are present in popular culture and literature. He offers insight into the significance and meaning of mythology's inclusion, and guides the reader to recognize myth and understand its meaning. [iii]

The body of scholarly critical literature devoted to "The Lord of the Rings" and "Harry Potter" is enormous. Anne Petty for instance is a Tolkien scholar who focuses on mythology, and she has written several books including Tolkien in the Land of Heroes. In this book, she explores the imaginative world created by Tolkien and the themes that illustrate the human condition that are present in Tolkien's books. She discusses the link between the heroes and villians of Middle Earth and ancient archetypes, and she discusses how Tolkien created Middle Earth. [iv]

Tolkien Studies [v] is a yearly publication of scholarly Tolkien related articles on a variety of subjects, including Tolkien's use of language, the creatures of Middle Earth, and mythology. Many of the articles on Tolkien's mythology focus on the Celtic mythological references in the books. [vi]

Likewise, many articles have been written on Rowling's series of books and her use of mythology. Many of these articles examine her inclusion of symbols, names, and creatures from mythology and define and discuss the mythological significance of their inclusion in the stories. In addition, many articles on Rowling's books focus on magic and its impact on young readers. [vii]

As the title implies, From Homer to Harry Potter [viii] by Matthew Dickerson examines fantasy literature through the centuries. It discusses the roots of modern fantasy, epic fantasy, fairy tales, and myths and legends and the significance of fantasy literature. There are references to both "The Lord of the Rings" and "Harry Potter" in the books, but they are not discussed side by side or compared.

Frodo and Harry [ix]by Ted Baehr examines the characters of Frodo Baggins and Harry Potter from the movies. It discusses the two characters side by side and looks specifically at the fantastic yet realistic world of Frodo and compares it to the magical world of Harry Potter. The book also discusses a variety of movies because it focuses on entertainment media as a whole and their impact on people's lives.

As a result of the popularity of Tolkien's and Rowling's series, many books have been written about the elements of mythology that are present in these books. The Magical Worlds of The Lord of the Rings and The Magical Worlds of Harry Potter [x]by David Colbert each discuss the particulars of the books, including where the authors derived the names for characters, mythological connections, and symbolism. He provides an abundance of facts for readers to help them discover the deeper meaning of the books.[xi] Understanding the deeper meaning behind literature is important for adults and children. Mythology connects us to the past and is relevant to us in our daily lives.

CHAPTER II

THE IMPORTANCE OF MYTHOLOGY AND
LITERATURE TO ANCIENT CULTURES

Writing and the Development of Literature

Written language was a vital step in the development of humans because it allowed thoughts, ideas and myths to be more efficiently preserved and transmitted to future generations.

The Minoan civilization on the Aegean island of Crete emerged approximately 2000 B.C. The Minoans were an advanced civilization that had indoor plumbing, sophisticated art, division of labor and a trade organization. Minoan civilization was wealthy because of agriculture and sea trade with people from around the Mediterranean and with Egypt. As a result of the need to record transactions, they developed Linear A, an early form of writing used primarily for accounting purposes.

The Mycenaeans formed the next great Western civilization in approximately 1500 B.C. in an area that soon became known as Greece. This was the civilization of Homer's heroes: Agamemnon, Achilles, and the heroic Greeks who defeated the Trojans. Thomas Cahill, author of <u>Sailing the Wine-Dark Sea,</u> states that it is the stories of the great Mycenaean age that "were preserved as oral poetry by wandering bards and written down only much later when a far more flexible form of writing came into currency that permitted the recording of epics of massive length and graceful

15

subtlety" (19-20). The Mycenaeans also developed a form of writing, designated Linear B, and the Mycenaeans became so powerful in the region that the Minoans converted to using Linear B for accounting.

In the late eighth century B.C., a new innovative form of writing began to develop in Greece. Over time, the Greeks adopted symbols for vowels to augment the consonants so eventually an alphabet was developed. Early writing systems were primarily used for accounting purposes, but the development of a Greek alphabet "announced a civilization of leisure…and it has long been understood that a fully articulated alphabet served as the medium for the gradual democratizing of the ancient societies in which it was introduced and took hold" (Cahill 58). Once an alphabet was developed it was easier to record thoughts, history, stories, and laws.

In ancient Greece, works of literature, such as Homer's The Iliad and The Odyssey were recorded in the 8th century B.C.; yet, because of the method of recording they were impractical for ownership by the common man. Literary works were preserved in several ways, including scratching the words "onto sheets of lead, or, in the case of especially valued monumental inscriptions, impressed on gold, or bronze, or carved in stone" (Cahill 84). Gradually, other book making methods were developed and books became more widely available. In Rome, during the period of the Republic, some wealthy individuals owned a small number of literary works that were often made available to the owner's circle of friends, but public libraries were not established until centuries later. The limited availability of literary works and a population that was largely illiterate meant that until better methods of writing and recording were developed, ancient society was largely "a hearing public" not a reading public (Cahill 85).

The Greek society of the Classical period was the first democratic society in the world. It was a golden age of civilization that emphasized education and led to the emergence of books. The result was a shift from a hearing public to a literary public. Early authors, such as Homer wrote in poetic form and Thomas Cahill believes that the fact that Aristotle and Plato wrote in prose not poetry is "evidence that books were circulating widely in the Greek world" (157) during the Classical period. The circulation of books is important for the spreading of thoughts and ideas and the expansion of literacy and culture within a civilization.

Writing allowed people to express their opinions and tell their stories, and because of the stability and permanence of writing, the stories and ideas were preserved for future generations. When something is passed down orally it is changed with every telling, and over time it may no longer reflect the original idea. As a result, the original information is lost. However, when something is written down it can survive for years and pass on the original information to successive generations of people. Tolkien and Rowling were able to incorporate ancient Greco-Roman mythology into their stories because those stories had been preserved through the millennia because of writing.

Writing allowed democratic ideals to be permanently recorded and spread to others, and the freedom democracy afforded, allowed people to write and interpret literature freely without the infringement of the state. Cahill states that although the political innovation called democracy took shape two centuries after Homer's epics were written down, the soldiers' town meetings in The Iliad is "ample evidence that long before, Greeks in general were comfortable with a freedom of discussion unknown in other nations ... this freedom progressed virtually in tandem with another innovation of the late eighth century, the alphabet, which in its turn triggered the possibility of widespread literacy" (55). Therefore, it was a combination of many factors, including the development of writing, the development of recording methods, and democratization that allowed for freedom of expression and an open exchange of ideas that led to the development of literature.

Beginning with Homer, Greek and Roman literature included stories about the gods and about the feats of humans and was rich in mythology. Homer, the legendary storyteller of ancient Ionia who lived in the late eighth and early seventh centuries B.C. is credited with being the first author of Western literature. Scholars have debated whether Homer was one person, or if the works attributed to Homer were actually the product of several people, but regardless, Homer owes a debt to the centuries of unwritten storytelling tradition that came before him. The stories were told and retold and "remolded over many generations by wandering bards until one of them, a man known to us by his name, but by no other solid biographical facts, gave them at last a highly selective and definitive treatment in two epic renderings in the very period that alphabetical writing was spreading across the Greek world" (Cahill 61).

The Iliad tells the story of the Trojan War which lasted ten years and the Greeks' efforts to free the beautiful Helen who was lured away from her home by the Trojan Paris. The Odyssey tells the story of the Greek hero and warrior Odysseus, his ten-year journey home from the Trojan War, and his fight to reclaim his title and estate. Throughout his adventure, Odysseus faces many physical and psychological challenges that test his abilities. He suffers, yet endures, and he eventually returns home only to have to fight to reclaim what is rightfully his. The Iliad and The Odyssey were the first pieces of Western literature. However, to the ancient Greeks the stories were history and people believed they were the stories of the Golden Age of long ago, a time when the gods still visited Earth and concerned themselves with human affairs.

Greek Mythology

The ancient Greeks developed an elaborate agglomeration of myths that formed the basis of a society that influenced the development of later civilizations in the Western world. During the Classical period, from 500 B.C. to 323 B.C., many aspects of our modern belief systems were first established, and a foundation of thought was begun which would inspire modern civilization. Greek mythology explained the world and man's place in the world to individual members of ancient society, and it has continued to influence western culture and literature into modern times.

Storytelling entertained and educated ancient people. Listening to stories told by the elders was the equivalent of the first classroom. Communally, people learned about life and the accomplishments of the people who came before them. The stories were passed down to the next generation to explain the world around them. The Greek myths illustrate passion, fallibility, and the joys of humanity. They explore every human emotion including laughter, love, anger, and jealousy, and through the myths, people recognize the continuity of human experiences. Generation after generation returns to mythology because of the universal truths they contain and their symbolic relevance to modern lives. Although people may not fight a Cyclops or travel to Hades, everyone faces monsters and fears, and by reading myths we gain strength through the struggles and perseverance of the heroes, the gods and goddesses, and the mortals of the stories.

The gods and goddesses of Greek Mythology are anthropocentric unlike the animal deities of the Egyptians and Mesopotamians. The Greeks were the first to put humans at the center of the universe and this is one important aspect of the Greek worldview. The Greek gods and goddesses not only physically resemble humans but they possess the emotional flaws of humans as well. The Greek gods and goddesses are often petty, jealous, caring, and loving just like humans. They are not infallible so they sometimes make mistakes. They also interfere in human lives sometimes bringing tragedy but also providing wisdom and compassion.

Before there was scientific knowledge to explain the formation of the world and the creation of mankind there were creation myths. The ancient Greek creation myth begins with chaos and darkness. Later, out of the swirling energy came Gaia, Mother Earth, who created the mountains, rivers, deserts, and oceans. In addition came Uranus, the heavens, who created the animals and birds of the Earth. Together, they had twelve children known as the Titans. Cronus, the youngest Titan, hated his father and finally overthrew him. Cronus married Rhea, also a Titan, and together they had children, but Cronus learned of a prophecy that one day one of his children would overthrow him, so when each child was born he devoured it. Rhea, his wife, was heartbroken and with Gaia's help the sixth time she gave birth, Rhea wrapped up a rock in swaddling clothes and presented it to the unknowing Cronus, who swallowed it. The child Zeus was hidden and when Zeus grew up he tricked his father into drinking a potion that made Cronus cough up his other children: Demeter, Hera, Hades, Hestia, and Poseidon. Together, Zeus and his siblings overthrew the Titans including Cronus. Zeus and his brothers and sisters then took their place as the gods and goddesses on Mount Olympus. Later, Prometheus, a Titan who fought by Zeus' side against Cronus, made mortal beings from clay. His brother Epimetheus had already given many of the gifts, such as strength, speed, and stealth to the animals on Earth so Prometheus decided to give men fire to protect them.

Zeus was furious and decided to cause trouble for humans. He sent Pandora to Epimetheus, who told Pandora not to open a particular jar. However, because she was curious she opened it, and all sorts of ills were released into the world. However, hope did not escape and was left in the jar to help mankind.[xii]

Nature myths were developed as a way to educate people in the changing of the seasons. The myth of Demeter and Persephone is the Greek version of why the seasons change. Demeter, the goddess of grain and the harvest, was responsible for the success of the crops. Her daughter Persephone was the maiden of spring, and when Hades, ruler of the underworld kidnapped Persephone and made her his bride, Demeter fell into a deep depression and the Earth turned cold and barren. The people of Earth suffered because while Demeter was sad nothing grew. Finally, Zeus intervened and sent Hermes to find a compromise. Hades agreed to send Persephone back to her mother. However, because Persephone ate a pomegranate seed while in the underworld she had to return to Hades part of each year. Consequently, when Persephone returns to the underworld winter comes to the Earth because Demeter is sad, but when Persephone returns to her mother spring comes and the flowers once again bloom. [xiii]

Heroic myths educate people in the social order of society, the perseverance of the human spirit, and the deeds of individuals. Heroes, such as Theseus, Hercules, Jason, and Odysseus are inspiring because they outwit and defeat hideous monsters, and they overcome their inner fears, insecurities, and other flaws. The monsters themselves "represent the destructive forces that people meet in their lives, such as disease, famine, and flood" (Randall 84). The heroes struggle with feelings that everyone struggles with, such as fear, jealousy, anger, and greed, and they successfully overcome those feelings and triumph. Heroes are role models for people and show that the "human spirit at its best can overcome almost any problem" (Randall 84). This is a lesson that is important to people as they struggle with personal problems and obstacles.

Major Gods and Goddesses of Mythology

Greek	Roman	God/Goddess of
Aphrodite	Venus	Goddess of beauty and love
Ares	Mars	God of war
Artemis	Diana	Goddess of hunting and childbirth
Athena	Minerva	Goddess of war and wisdom
Demeter	Ceres	Goddess of the harvest
Hera	Juno	Goddess of marriage
Hermes	Mercury	Messenger of the gods
Hades	Pluto	God of the Underworld
Poseidon	Neptune	God of the sea
Zeus	Jupiter	King of the gods, God of the sky

Mythology's Importance in Ancient Greek Life

Epic poems that contained myths were recited or acted out in theatrical performances as a means of education and entertainment. Epics are "a long narrative poem in elevated style presenting characters of high position in adventures forming an organic whole through their relation to a central heroic figure and through their development of episodes important to the history of a nation or race" (Harmon 185). Epic poems taught the audience lessons about life, such as man's relationship to the gods, they taught cultural values, such as the guest – host relationship and fidelity, and they provided examples of heroism and quality of character for the audience. Because the stories were part of the education process, the audience knew the stories well, and they became part of humankind's collective knowledge and history.

The lessons learned from mythology vary with the person reading it and the age in which it is read. Perception and interpretation of literature is dependent on the personality of the reader and the social and economic events of the time. The Greeks of the Classical period believed in the existence of the gods, so to them the stories had religious significance. Ancient people worried about angering the gods, about the occurrence of natural disasters, and the causes of natural events, such as eclipses. They did not understand nature and they did not have safety nets, such as governmental assistance for difficult times. If the crop failed – the family starved. Help only came from generous friends and neighbors. In Art and Experience in Classical Greece author J.J. Pollitt says that because of the uncertainties of life, the Greeks had an exceptionally "deep seated need to discover an order in, or superimpose an order on, the flux of physical and psychological experience" (3). The Greeks sought "recognition of order and measure in phenomena which did more than simply satisfy their intellectual curiosity or gratify a desire for tidiness; it also served as that basis of a spiritual ideal" (Pollitt 4) for society.

Classical Greek society was a group-centered society. An individual was expected to "merge his life and interests with those of the group" (Pollitt 10). Because the ancient Greeks believed that one individual could bring down the wrath of the gods on the entire community, Greek society emphasized moderation, restraint, and the avoidance of hubris, or excess pride because they feared a return to chaos and uncertainty. Moderation became a key aspect of life for some ancient Greek philosophers such as Aristotle, who is the "Father of Virtue Ethics".

Virtue Ethics is a philosophical approach to morality that emphasizes the midpoint or balance, the Mean, between the Vices of excess and deficiency. To have excessive pride in oneself and one's community is to have hubris which is a Vice. The lack of pride in oneself and one's community is a deficiency which is also a Vice. The midpoint or balance, the Mean, is to have pride in oneself and one's community but not to have so much pride that one forgets his or her place in society. Only when a person is virtuous and achieves balance in life has the individual achieved the goal of Virtue Ethics: Happiness. Aristotle's ethical system can be described as "eminently common-sense-based…[founded] on the moral judgments of the ideal human being, who based upon reason, is considered good and virtuous" (Thiroux and Krasemann 71). Therefore, in order for a person to achieve this goal, the individual must come to know and understand him or herself very well.

The entrance to Apollo's Temple at Delphi, one of the most sacred temples in the ancient world and home to the Oracle of Delphi to whom people traveled to receive her predictions, is inscribed with the words, "Know Thyself". These words mean know your limitations and do nothing to excess. Pollitt says, "all Greeks were subject to and respected the maxims of the Delphic oracle" (11) because the oracle was part of the religious tradition just as myth was a part of the religious tradition. "Know Thyself" also represents the idea that man must achieve balance in life, and to achieve balance moderation is always best. However, achieving balance is not always easy as illustrated in the drama and literature of the period.

Mythology's Importance in Drama and Literature

Greek drama was first developed in Athens in the 6th century B.C. It often contained mythology and it taught the population the lessons of life. In the Poetics, Aristotle defined tragedy as "an imitation of an action that is admirable, complete and possesses magnitude; in language made pleasurable, each of its species separated in different parts; performed by actors, not through narration; effecting through pity and fear the purification of such emotions" (10). Tragedies interpret the ancient myths and concern "a limited number of families" (Aristotle 24) who have significance in Greek history. However, tragedies are not history because history deals with a particular and tragedy deals with the generic. Unlike history, tragedy reveals "what is possible in accordance with probability or necessity" (Aristotle 16). In watching a tragedy, the audience connects the generic issue presented in the play to a specific contemporary event.

Tragedies were significant in that they made people reflect on their lives and their behaviors. The plots of tragedies were "based on stories that harkened back to a time before the polis, [however], the tales of the Trojan War and the moral issues illuminated by the plays always pertained to the society and obligation of citizens in a polis" (Martin 132). Pollitt states,

> The best dramas bring into focus simultaneously most of the intellectual and emotional preoccupations of the early Classical period – the willingness to believe that there is a meaningful moral order in the world, the consequent uneasiness over the human tendency to pursue self interest through violence, the possible implications of such violence within the moral order, the new significance attached to individual human consciousness and thought, and finally a new conception of what constitutes nobility in human character" (27).

28

Drama was performed for a largely non-reading public as part of religious festivals, such as the Dionysia, an important spring festival in honor of Dionysus, the god of wine. One of Aeschylus' trilogies, The Oresteia, illustrates the contemporary shift in philosophy because the old ways are swept away and replaced by new ways governed by order and justice. The plays also incorporate the gods and mythology, and are an important link to tradition and the religious beliefs of society. At the end of "The Eumenides," the third part of the trilogy, the goddess Athene brings twelve men from Athens to her temple to participate in the trial of Orestes who has been charged with matricide. After the evidence is presented, Orestes is acquitted, and Athene tells the men of Athens, "I establish this tribunal. It shall be untouched by money-making, grave but quick to wrath, watchful to protect those who sleep, a sentry of the land" (Aeschylus 704-6). The cycle of violence and eye for an eye mentality of the old order of society is swept away and replaced with a new order that is based on justice, order and rational behavior. By teaching men how to conduct a trial, Athene takes power of justice away from the few who rule and puts it into the hands of the people. This is an allegory of Athenian society that at the time was moving away from an oligarchy, rule of the few, toward a democracy, rule by the people, and reaffirms the Greek confidence in their society.

To ancient people these stories were more than entertainment. The stories reflected historical and current affairs in Greece and they had religious significance. Through drama, knowledge was conveyed and people studied and learned the old stories so they could in turn pass on the knowledge to the next generation.

Transmission of Greek Mythology

Western civilization derives its inspiration, theories, and political structure from the ancient Greeks. Frederick Copleston in <u>A History of Philosophy</u> states, "no one would attempt to deny that the Greeks left an imperishable legacy of literature and art to our European world" (10). Although Eastern traders brought goods to Greece and exposed the Greeks to new concepts, such as Eastern mathematics, languages, philosophy, myths, and rituals we must "not underestimate the originality of the Greek mind" (11). The Greeks had a unique civilization and "stand as the uncontested original thinkers and scientists of Europe" (Copleston 16). Joseph Campbell agrees with Copleston that the Greeks were original thinkers because at a time when other cultures were addressing "animal, plant, cosmic and super natural orders . . . in Greece, already in the period of Homer, the world had become man's world" ("Myths" 58). As early as the eighth century B.C. Greeks were already beginning to look at the world through the human perspective.

Greek culture, especially in the areas of mythology, religion, literature, art, and architecture, had the most profound influence on Roman society. The Greek influence on the Romans is evident in the story of Aeneas that links the founding of Rome to the destruction of the legendary city of Troy. According to myth, Aeneas, the son of the goddess Venus, escapes from Troy with his father Anchises. Aeneas makes his way to Latium, where he marries into the royal family and his wife gives birth to twin boys, Romulus and Remus. Years later, Romulus kills his brother and founds Rome thus becoming Rome's first king. [xiv]

The Romans, known as the great assimilators because they accepted people other than Romans into the Republic, allowed conquered people to continue practicing traditional customs and beliefs and often adopted other cultures' traditions into their own. In Roman Society, Henry C. Boren states that Roman citizens routinely came "into contact with new concepts and new cults" (81) as the Republic expanded and included a variety of people from different cultures. He further states, "Rome was relatively tolerant of religious innovation" (Boren 81). Romans "identified their gods with those of the Greeks and adopted the Greek myths as their own" (Boren 14). Therefore, much of Roman culture is derived from Greek models, and because of the tremendous and lasting influence of the Roman Empire on Western civilization Greek mythology has been transmitted through the centuries to modern people.

The Relevance of Ancient Civilization to Modern Society

The safest general characterization of the European philosophical tradition is that it consists of a series of footnotes to Plato. - Alfred North Whitehead (Ner Le'Elef 118)

The importance of the ancient Greeks and Romans cannot be denied because the foundation of Western society and culture, its customs, myths, and form of government can be traced directly to the two civilizations. The Greeks' victory over the Persians was vital to the formation of Western civilization because without the victory there would not have been a golden age of Greek civilization, and Western mythology might have been lost. The victory quickened the pace of changes already underway in society, specifically the formation of a democratic form of government. In addition, the victory boosted Greek confidence in society and led to a period of growth, building, and philosophy that had never before been seen in the world. The victory was vital because if the Greeks had lost to the invading Persians and "had Greece become just another province of the empire there would have been no brilliant Athenian century to serve as the foundation of modern culture" (Headden 8). Key battles, such as Thermopylae, Salamis, and Marathon boosted Greek confidence and were critical battles in the defeat of the Persians.

At Thermopylae, the Greeks lost. However, the Spartan army managed to hold off the larger Persian army for several days, and they lost only after a Greek betrayed the Spartans and showed the Persians a way around the pass. This was a tremendous achievement for the smaller Greek force and it illustrates the resolve of the Greek people. They were determined to not become part of the Persian Empire and thereby lose their freedom and their right to self-government.

At Salamis, the smaller Greek, primarily Athenian, fleet successfully defeated the larger Persian fleet by using the topography of the land and superior military tactics. The battle at Salamis in 480 B.C. was a critical victory for the Greeks because it turned the tide of the war in favor of the Greeks. The naval encounter was "the supreme confrontation between east and west, in which all manner of futures were either set in motion or denied" (Hanson 15). The victory dealt a blow to the Persians, fortified Greek confidence, and ensured the survival of Greek society.

In contrast to the orderly Greeks was the Persian society that encompassed many cultures and people and had a large economic gap between those who ruled and the governed. The Persian leader, Xerxes, is "the anti-Greek, the man of unlimited power who is subject to no restraint, no limit to desire, the man who does whatever he wants whenever a whim demands it" (Pollitt 14). When the ordered and rational Greeks defeated the chaotic Persians, Greek confidence in their society increased and led to "the belief that men could shape their world in accordance with their own vision of it" (Pollitt 64). In addition, "there was an anthropocentric drift in Greek philosophy away from concern with the physical world and toward a preoccupation with human society" (Pollitt 64). The Greeks strove for order to alleviate anxiety and the victory over the Persians reaffirmed Greek abilities, gave confidence to the society, and caused them to focus on the achievements of men.

The Greek defeat of the Persians signals a shift from doubt to confidence in society. With newfound confidence and the belief that the victory proves that Greek society is a just society, the Greeks began rebuilding temples and structures destroyed in the war against Persia. Although the peace did not last long and Athens entered into a war with their one time ally, Sparta, the determination and confidence of the Athenians was still strong and sustained them for many years, and led to a variety of new innovations.

The Classical period was the time when democracy developed and people began to understand that they had the power to shape the world and they had the confidence to exert their will on the Universe. One outcome of the Greeks confidence during the Classical period was the development of man centered philosophy proposed by Protagoras of Abdera who believed truth is found within the man and man has the ability to change his future. Protagoras, "the father of relativism" (Fearn 10) proclaimed, "Man is the measure of all things". This philosophy is based on the belief that the way man perceives something determines the reality of it. Therefore, a person's perception of something makes it reality for that individual. The Greeks believed that humanity was important and this humanistic view of the world "led the Greeks to create the concept of democracy (rule by the demos, the people), and to make seminal contributions in the fields of art, literature, and science" (Kleiner 91). The combination of a new radical philosophy of life, a rich mythology, and the freedom that democracy affords culminated in creating a society unlike any the world had ever seen, and one that would inspire later civilizations beginning with the Romans.

If the Greeks lost the war with Persia, Westerners would be living in a very different world today. The Persians wanted to stop the advance of Western culture because concepts such as equality did not conform to Eastern hierarchical society at the time. The ancient Greeks were a unique people because "the words freedom and citizen did not exist in the vocabulary of any other Mediterranean culture" (Hanson 19). Much of Western society derives inspiration from the Athenian society established after the defeat of the Persians and if the Persians had prevailed there would have been no "Athenian tragedy and comedy, no Socratic philosophy" (Hanson 17), no democracy, and no Greek mythology.

The 5th century B.C. was a Golden Age for the Greeks in Athens who established the world's first democracy, transformed art and architecture, developed a radical philosophy of life based on human perceptions, and gave the world tragedy. In a free society people can formulate a variety of thoughts and ideas free from the constraints of a totalitarian ruler. Athenian democracy and culture was "the catalyst for a subsequent literary, artistic and philosophical explosion" (Hanson 17) which shaped and defined Western culture. Therefore, "our democratic form of government, our clean and elegant forms of architecture, and tragedy and comedy on stage" (Headden 5) are all inherited from 5th century Athenian society after the victory over the Persians.

At about the same time that Greece was undergoing a radical transformation, the Romans were establishing a Republic, another form of democratic government. The Romans adopted many aspects of Greek culture that they then spread across the Western world, and in the process the Romans preserved the culture for future generations.

The Greeks were a powerful influence on Roman society in all areas of culture, including literature, theater, art and architecture, philosophy and religion. The Romans "identified their gods with those of the Greeks and adopted the Greek myths as their own" (Boren 14). The Roman gods are identical to Greek gods, but with different names. For example, the Greek god Zeus is Jupiter to the Romans, and Athena is the Roman goddess

Minerva. Herakles, Hercules to the Romans, is probably the greatest Greek hero. The son of Zeus and a mortal woman, Herakles, had to complete twelve great labors as retribution for killing his wife and children after Hera, Zeus' wife, made him go mad. The adoption of Greek myths by the Romans is illustrated in the triumph of Hercules (Herakles) that is depicted on a Roman sarcophagus on display at the Museum of Fine Art in Boston.

In addition, the Romans contributed their own unique elements, such as the law, the idea of a constitution, and road construction techniques to Western society. Rome was very liberal in granting citizenship to conquered people and many aspects of a conquered people's culture were assimilated into Roman society. Colonies and garrisons established throughout the Republic then spread Roman beliefs and culture to other newly conquered people. Therefore, there was a mixing of cultures that spread across a vast part of the Western world that continued long after Rome became an Empire, and because of Rome's longevity, many aspects of cultures long conquered endured and were transmitted down through the centuries.

One ideology that survived the centuries is democracy, or rule of the people. To be an Athenian or Roman citizen meant there were obligations to religion and government, but it also meant there were many rewards, and citizenship was a source of pride. In both societies, all citizens, regardless of wealth, were expected to participate in running the government. In the Roman government, offices were filled by elections, but the Athenians believed everyone should participate, and so they filled government offices by lot. Athenians believed it was every citizen's moral obligation to participate in governing the polis to the extent the individual's talents allow. Pericles declared in his Funeral Oration, "Here each individual is interested not only in his own affairs, but in the affairs of the state as well ... this is a peculiarity of ours: we do not say that a man who takes no interest in politics is a man who minds his own business; we say he has no business here at all" (Thucydides 147). A government made up of citizens was a revolutionary idea that the colonists of America embraced over 2,000 years later.

The achievements of the Greeks and Romans were so important that Greek, Latin, and Biblical literature are often taught in school, even in public school. Ancient stories help people make decisions and provide perspective on what is happening today. Loss of the information puts people at a disadvantage. The importance of the old stories should not be underestimated because "these bits of information from ancient times, which have to do with the themes that have supported human life, built civilizations and informed religions over the millennia, have to do with deep inner problems, inner mysteries, inner thresholds of passage, and if you don't know what the guide-signs are along the way, you have to work it out yourself" (Campbell 'Power of Myth" 2). Myths are man's stories about life and how the universe works, myths help people understand the inner meaning of life, and they link people to their cultural past.

A basic understanding of Greek and Roman mythology is necessary to fully understand and appreciate many works of Western literature because references to myths are found in many works of literature. Myths "remain the basis of our fiction" and we cannot study literature without them (Frye "Biblical and Classical Myths" 277). Homer's works are considered by Cahill and most literary scholars to be "the foundation masterpiece of western literature" because they "are hybrids: literate works that are profoundly influenced by many previous generations of oral transmission" (22, 60-1). The interpretation of Homer's works varies throughout the centuries, yet "every age has found relevance for its own time" (Cahill 41).

Homer's works establish literary archetypes, such as the hero archetype and the journey archetype that are represented by Odysseus. These archetypes and others serve as a template for many works of literature through the centuries including modern children's literature such as "The Lord of the Rings" and "Harry Potter".

CHAPTER III

THE HERO AND THE JOURNEY

The Heroes: Odysseus to Harry

In <u>The Iliad</u> and <u>The Odyssey</u>, Homer's epic heroic character Odysseus is the model for the literary archetype of the hero and the journey. Odysseus has flaws as all heroes do, but he strives to do what is right and exemplifies the strength of humans.

The hero and journey archetypes established by Homer have come down to modern times through centuries of authors who used the archetype for their own stories. Some of these stories include <u>Beowulf</u>, a quasi-epic poem that chronicles the adventures of the larger than life hero, Beowulf, who journeys to distant lands to do battle with the monsters Grendel and Grendel's mother and then returns home. The author of <u>Beowulf</u> is unknown and the earliest surviving manuscript from approximately 1400 is housed at the British Museum in London and is considered to be an archeological relic. Scholars believe the poem was originally written in "the eighth century A.D." and reflects the "rigid feudal, highly civilized, and highly violent and rather newly Christian" society in England at the time (Raffel xi).

<u>Sir Gawain and the Green Knight</u> was written in the fourteenth century in England and is the story of one of King Arthur's Knights of the Round Table. Also written by an anonymous author, Sir Gawain is a noble knight in King Arthur's court who accepts the challenge of the mysterious

Green Knight and cuts off the knight's head with a single blow. The Green Knight picks up his severed head and announces that Gawain must meet him on the next New Year's Day to receive the same blow. Gawain is an honorable knight, so as the New Year approaches, Gawain journeys to the Green Knight's castle, and along the way he must battle an ogre, a dragon, and a pack of wolves. He must also resist the Lady of the house at which he stays. When Sir Gawain finally faces the Green Knight again he learns that the challenge was not a trial of strength, but a trial of honor.

Other stories that incorporate the mythic hero and journey archetypes include the epic poem The Divine Comedy also written in the fourteenth century. It is written in three parts: "Inferno", "Purgatorio", and "Paradisio." In each section Dante the poet recounts the travels of the Pilgrim protagonist as he journeys through hell, purgatory, and heaven. Moby Dick written in 1851 by Herman Melville is the epic tale of Captain Ahab of the whaling ship the Pequod, who relentlessly pursues the great sperm whale Moby Dick that serves as a metaphor for a distorted quest. Mark Twain's Huckleberry Finn written in 1884 is the coming of age story of Huck, a young man who runs away from civilization in pursuit of freedom. Through Huck's journey the novel explores issues, such as racism and morality. James Joyce's Ulysses written in 1922 is an epic length novel that chronicles the journey of the main character Leopold Bloom through an ordinary day in Dublin with many implicit and explicit parallels between the novel and The Odyssey.

J.R.R. Tolkien penned The Hobbit in 1937 about Bilbo Baggins' adventure through Middle Earth to help a group of dwarves restore their kingdom and find the great treasure stolen by Smaug the dragon. While on the adventure Bilbo encounters a strange creature and acquires a mysterious ring. Tolkien's high fantasy epic adventure "The Lord of the Rings", written in 1954, is a continuation of the story begun in <u>The Hobbit</u>. It chronicles Frodo Baggins' quest to destroy Bilbo's ring which is revealed to be the Ring of Power that will destroy Middle Earth. J.K. Rowling's the Harry Potter series is one of the newest installments of the hero and journey archetype and details Harry's adventures at Hogwarts School of Witchcraft and Wizardry.

Over the millennia many stories have incorporated the hero and journey archetypes developed so long ago by Homer, and all these stories illustrate the power of good over evil and the strength of human beings.

The Hero and the Journey Archetypes in Literature

Throughout history, authors, including J.R.R. Tolkien and J.K. Rowling have used literary archetypes as a means of structuring their stories and by their inclusion the stories have been made more complex and interesting. It is not coincidental that many authors are scholars or students of mythology who infuse their stories with myths and references to myths. J.R.R. Tolkien was an Oxford professor and scholar of mythology and languages. He translated works into English, and produced one of the first modern translations of Sir Gawain and the Green Knight. J.K. Rowling is also a scholar of mythology who earned degrees in French and Classics from Exeter University. She first came up with the idea for Harry while on a train ride and wrote the first book over several years. Both authors draw on their considerable knowledge of mythology and use the hero and the journey archetypes to tell their stories.

In literature, heroes are important and interesting characters who set an example for others and who teach the reader that there are more important things in life than personal gain. In hero stories, the "hero goes out to accomplish something" (Frye "Myth" 213). The hero is not simply out for adventure but is on a quest. Joseph Campbell maps the hero character in his book The Hero With A Thousand Faces. Campbell defines the mythological hero's journey as a circle. The hero leaves home naïve and immature and he or she returns home older, wiser, and stronger because of the challenges that were faced along the way. A wise helper usually appears to the hero at the beginning of the journey and provides guidance and advice to the hero along the way. On the journey, the hero faces an assortment of physical and mental challenges, some of which put the hero's life in danger. Finally, the hero "arrives at the nadir of the mythological round, he undergoes a supreme ordeal and gains his reward" (Campbell "Hero" 246). Once the hero's mission is accomplished he "re-emerges from the kingdom of dread and the boon that he brings restores the world" (Campbell "Hero" 246). The hero is someone who embarks on the journey without regard for personal safety, but embarks on the journey only to save others.

The Basics of the Hero and Journey Archetype

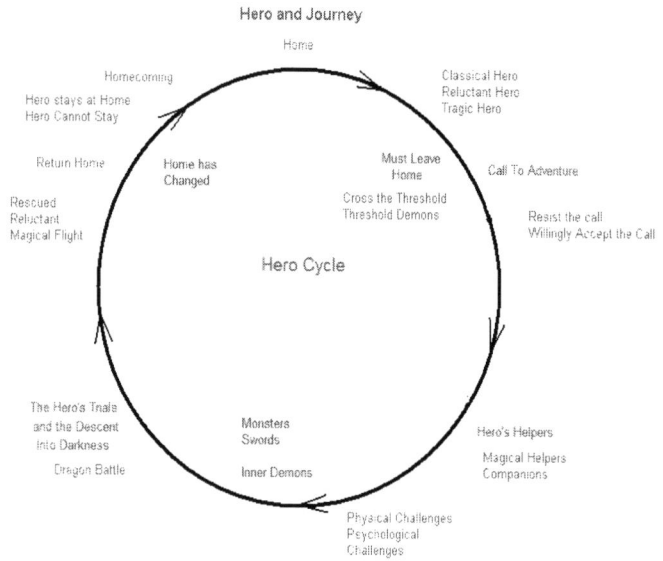

Hero and Journey

Home

Homecoming

Hero stays at Home
Hero Cannot Stay

Classical Hero
Reluctant Hero
Tragic Hero

Return Home

Home has
Changed

Must Leave
Home

Call To Adventure

Rescued
Reluctant
Magical Flight

Cross the Threshold
Threshold Demons

Resist the call
Willingly Accept the Call

Hero Cycle

The Hero's Trials
and the Descent
Into Darkness

Monsters
Swords

Hero's Helpers

Magical Helpers
Companions

Dragon Battle

Inner Demons

Physical Challenges
Psychological
Challenges

The Predestined Hero and Fate

The archetype of the hero usually involves a predestined hero who has hidden exceptional abilities. Theseus is a predestined hero because he is the son of King Aegeus and an Oracle prophesied his birth. Odysseus is predestined because he is the leader of Ithaca and is therefore a person of significance. Frodo Baggins is predestined because his call to adventure is prophesied in a dream. "Isildur's Bane shall waken, and the Halfling forth shall stand" (Tolkien "Fellowship" 276). The hereditary predestined hero like Frodo is commonly found throughout literature.

Often the hero is the nephew because of the important roles that uncles played in the family. Custom "required that uncles play the role of guardian, in case a father died early (as often happened)". (Colbert 9) One legendary nephew is Sir Gawain, the nephew of King Arthur, who is also one of the Knights of the Round Table. Another example is Beowulf, who was the nephew of the king. Nephews often became "as great or greater than their uncles" (Colbert 9) in legends and inspired their own stories. In his book The Magical Worlds of The Lord of the Rings David Colbert says Tolkien originally planned for Bilbo to continue his adventure after The Hobbit but later chose to make the hero "a younger cousin, with the official status of nephew and heir [because] it was time for a new hero." (Colbert 10) Bilbo leaves everything to Frodo when he departs for Rivendell, including the golden ring, the Ring of Power.

Harry Potter is also predestined because of a prophecy. Shortly before Harry's birth, a Seer foretold of the birth of a child who would defeat Lord Voldemort. "The one with the power to vanquish the Dark Lord approaches... Born to those who have thrice defied him, Born as the seventh month dies... And the Dark Lord will mark him as his equal." (Rowling "Order" 841) When Voldemort attacked Harry, Harry became the predestined hero of the prophecy.

The hero often exhibits powers greater than others, yet the power is not necessarily only physical strength. Joseph Campbell states that the makers of legend often "endowed the hero with extraordinary powers ... and the whole hero-life is shown to have been a pageant of marvels with the great central adventure as its culmination" ("Hero" 319). There are several examples of predestined heroes who have exceptional mental and physical abilities. Hercules, the son of Zeus, was born with exceptional strength and uses his strength to chop off each of the Hydra's heads, but strength is not enough to defeat the monster. Hercules must devise a strategy to keep the head from growing back so he can ultimately defeat the creature. Odysseus uses his formidable physical strength to ultimately defeat the Cyclops, but first he must devise a plan to trick the Cyclops into moving the massive boulder that blocks the exit from the cave in which Odysseus and his men are trapped.

Frodo has a remarkable ability to resist the Ring's power, at least at first. Elrond tells Boromir at the Council of Elrond in Rivendell that the Ring "is too great for anyone to wield at will, save only those who have already a great power of their own" (Tolkien "Fellowship" 300). Even Galadriel and Gandalf cannot take the Ring because the Ring can overpower them and force them to do terrible things. Frodo has the power because he has no desire to rule people. Gandalf tells Frodo, "you have been chosen, and you must therefore use such strength and heart and wits as you have" (Tolkien "Fellowship" 67). Frodo uses his wits when dealing with everyone he encounters, including Gollum, because the Ring will try to corrupt anyone it comes near. For example, Gollum wants to swear his allegiance to Frodo on the Ring that will bind him to his promise, but Frodo tells him, "All you wish is to see it and touch it...swear by it, if you will." (Tolkien "Towers" 249). Frodo knows if Gollum sees the Ring he will be unable to resist its power.

Harry Potter acquired some of his exceptional powers when he was an infant because Lord Voldemort's curse backfired and, instead of killing Harry, some of Lord Voldemort's powers were transferred to him. Dumbledore explains to Harry, "You can speak Parseltongue [ability to speak to snakes], Harry, because Lord Voldemort...can speak Parseltongue... he [Lord Voldemort] transferred some of his own powers to you the night he gave you that scar." (Rowling "Chamber" 332-3) Harry exhibits magical abilities far above his classmates. For example, when Harry had his first flying lesson the "broom jumped into his hand at once, but it was one of a few that did" (Rowling "Sorcerer" 146). Harry was immediately able to control his broom while other classmates struggled illustrating some of Harry's natural magical abilities. A few minutes later without ever having been on a broom before, he takes off after Draco Malfoy and makes a diving catch to save his friend Neville's Remembrall [a large marble sized ball that fills with red smoke when the owner has forgotten to do something]. In his third year at Hogwarts, Harry masters the Patronus Charm for repelling Dementors [faceless creatures that feed off fear] which is "highly advanced magic... well beyond Ordinary Wizarding Level" (Rowling "Prisoner" 237). Neither Frodo nor Harry fit the stereotype of the hero at the beginning of their journey, but once they accept their fate and the call to adventure, both exhibit tremendous strength of character and draw on inner abilities neither knew they possessed.

Fate was a powerful force to the ancient Greeks and Romans and they believed strongly in the role of fate. In The Iliad, Hector attempts to comfort his wife Andromache by telling her, "No man is going to hurl me to Hades, unless it is fated, / but as for fate I think that no man yet has escaped it" (Homer "Iliad" 487-88). In The Iliad, the hero Achilles knows that he will die if he fights at Troy, yet he accepts his fate and joins the fight because his companion Patroklos is killed.

Fate plays a role in "The Lord of the Rings" and "Harry Potter", and although fate is unavoidable, it does not necessarily rule the hero. Frodo is small, about the size of a child, he is always afraid, he is not strong, he is shy and quiet, and he does not want to carry the Ring. He says, "I am not made for perilous quests. I wish I had never seen the Ring! Why did it come to me? Why was I chosen?" (Tolkien "Fellowship" 67). However, it is Frodo's fate to carry the Ring as confirmed by Elrond who tells Frodo, "I think that this task is appointed for you, Frodo; and that if you do not find a way, no one will" (Tolkien "Fellowship" 303). Frodo is fated to carry the Ring because his heart is pure and he has no desire for power. Galadriel tells Frodo that the Ring gives "power according to the measure of each possessor." (Tolkien "Fellowship" 411) Therefore, because Frodo does not have the will to dominate over others he is therefore able to resist the power of the Ring.

Dumbledore tells Harry that it is his fate to fight Lord Voldemort. However, Dumbledore also tells Harry that it is the person's choices that set him or her apart from others. In book two, Harry comes face to face with a young Voldemort, and because Harry is believed to be the heir of Slytherin, he has an identity crisis. To complicate matters, the Sorting Hat, (the magical hat created by the four founders of Hogwarts that sorts incoming students into the four houses of the school), wanted to put Harry in Slytherin house, Lord Voldemort's house when he was a student at Hogwarts. The Sorting Hat did not put Harry in Slytherin House because Harry asked it not to. Dumbledore explains that it is a person's choices that make the individual unique and that "it is our choices...that show what we truly are" (Rowling "Chamber" 333). The fact that Harry asked the Sorting Hat not to put him in Slytherin House makes Harry different from Lord Voldemort even though Harry has some of the same abilities and powers as Voldemort.

The Call to Adventure

While some heroes accept the call to adventure and set out willingly to perform the deed prescribed by the journey, others are thrown into the adventure, and some heroes initially refuse the call. However, eventually something motivates the hero to change his or her mind. Once the call to adventure is accepted, the hero sets off on a series of extraordinary adventures.

The details vary, but ultimately the hero must move beyond the comfort and safety of home in order to undertake the journey. Theseus, the son of the king volunteers to be a sacrifice to the half-man half-bull Minotaur on the island of Crete in the hope of helping his people become free of the yearly ritual. Odysseus is thrust into the adventure because he did not show the proper piety to Poseidon, and therefore, like many protagonists in Greek literature, he must suffer for his hubris. Frodo and Harry embark on their dangerous journeys and accept their destiny and the call to adventure because of their morality and their desire to save their society.

Frodo risks his life to save the Shire and Middle Earth. Gandalf tells Frodo that the Enemy is "seeking for it [Ring] now" (Tolkien "Fellowship" 65). Frodo realizes the task is his destiny and that he must leave the Shire. He says, "I cannot keep the Ring and stay here. I ought to leave Bag End, leave the Shire, leave everything and go away…. I should like to save the Shire." (Tolkien "Fellowship" 68) When Frodo leaves the Shire he answers the call to adventure and takes the Ring to Rivendell where Frodo answers a second call to adventure. When the others cannot agree on who should take the Ring to Mordor, Frodo decides it is his calling and says, "I will take the Ring." (Tolkien "Fellowship" 303). He is not thinking about his own safety or personal welfare. His only concern is the Shire and the people of Middle Earth.

Harry also must answer the call to adventure because he wants to save the people and world that he loves from being overcome by evil. Harry faces Lord Voldemort several times through the course of the series and each time his life is at risk. Harry knows he must keep Voldemort from acquiring the Sorcerer's Stone because the Stone would return Voldemort to health. He says, "I'm going out of here tonight and I'm going to try and get to the Stone first" (Rowling "Sorcerer" 270). At the end of book six, Harry Potter and the Half-Blood Prince, Harry tells Ron and Hermione that he will not return to Hogwarts even if the school reopens in the fall because he has "to track down the rest of the Horcruxes... and destroy them" (Rowling 651). Harry comes to the realization that destroying Lord Voldemort is his calling and he knows that he must stop Voldemort no matter what the personal cost.

The heroes that accept the call to adventure are not perfect individuals. All heroes have flaws that they must overcome on their journey, but all are essentially good at heart. Frodo succumbs to the power of the Ring several times. Against Gandalf's advice, Frodo puts the Ring on at Weathertop because "his terror [at seeing the Ring Wraiths] was swallowed up in a sudden temptation to put on the Ring. The desire to do this laid hold of him, and he could think of nothing else" (Tolkien "Fellowship" 220). The king of the Ring Wraiths senses the Ring and stabs Frodo in the shoulder even though he is invisible causing a wound that will never fully heal. Near the end of the story, when standing in front of the fires of Mount Doom, Frodo once again gives in to the power of the Ring and puts it on. Frodo is able to resist the power of the Ring more than most but he does have lapses in control. However, Frodo has good intentions and he intends to destroy it for the good of all Middle Earth.

Harry too is imperfect and he makes mistakes. He breaks rules and acts impulsively, a point Professor Snape is always happy and quick to point out whenever Harry is caught doing something foolish or against the rules. At the beginning of <u>Harry Potter and the Chamber of Secrets</u>, Professor Snape emphasized the need for punishment for Harry and his friend Ron because they "Flounced the Decree for Restriction of Underage Wizardry, [and] caused serious damage to an old and valuable tree" (81) when the boys flew and crashed a magical car into a tree on their way to Hogwarts. Although Harry's behavior may not be exemplary, he has the best of intentions in his quest to destroy Voldemort and save the people and society he loves.

The Hero's Helpers

When heroes embark on the journey they usually have magical and wise helpers who will guide them along the way. According to the archetype of the hero, the Supernatural helper is "a protective figure" (Campbell "Heroes" 69) that teaches and guides the hero on his journey. Throughout the adventure, the hero is "covertly aided by the advice, amulets, and secret agents of the supernatural helper" (Campbell "Heroes" 97). The goddess Athene visits Odysseus several times on his journey home in The Odyssey. For example, Athene helps protect Odysseus when Poseidon is tossing him around the sea, and then she comes to him disguised as a young girl and shrouds him in a protective mist when he visits the king of the Phaeacians. Athene also helps Odysseus when he returns home by disguising him as an old man so he can ascertain the situation in his house and oust the suitors. Circe, one of Odysseus' supernatural guides tells Odysseus he and his crew must not listen to the Sirens' song as they sail past the cliffs. The Sirens are women whose singing makes men forget everything and they crash on the rocks and perish. Ariadne, the daughter of King Minos on Crete, aids Theseus in his quest to slay the Minotaur. She asks Dedalus, the creator of the maze in which the Minotaur is kept, for advice on how to help Theseus successfully navigate the maze.

In "The Lord of the Rings", Frodo has Gandalf the wizard to guide him on his quest to destroy the Ring. Gandalf leads Frodo and the Fellowship out of Rivendell and through Moria. He also provides psychological guidance and comfort, and tells Frodo, "I will always help you. I will help you bear this burden, as long as it is yours to bear" (Tolkien "Fellowship" 68).

Gandalf's agents also provide Frodo with help and advice. Gandalf tells Frodo in a letter, "you may meet a man on the Road: a Man, lean, dark, tall, by some called Strider. He knows our business and will help you" (Tolkien "Fellowship" 192 – 3). Strider is of course Aragorn the Ranger who helps Frodo and the Hobbits travel through the wilderness to Rivendell. Later, Frodo is also aided by Faramir, a student of Gandalf. He provides Frodo and Sam with food and water for their journey into Mordor and provides Frodo will valuable advice, "do not drink of any stream that flows from Imlad Morgul, the Valley of Living Death" (Tolkien "Towers" 341). Therefore, even when Gandalf cannot personally give advice and guidance his agents are there to help Frodo.

Harry Potter's guide and mentor is the powerful wizard Dumbledore who is headmaster of Hogwarts. At times Dumbledore uses magic to heal and save Harry, but he also provides guidance and emotional support. For example, at the end of The Goblet of Fire Dumbledore comforts Harry who has just witnessed his friend's murder and faced a fully restored Lord Voldemort. Voldemort attempted to kill Harry, but despite his young age and limited magical training Harry was able to escape death. Dumbledore tells Harry, "You have shouldered a grown wizard's burden and found yourself equal to it" (Rowling "Goblet" 699). Dumbledore is also a father figure to Harry because Harry is an orphan whose parents were murdered trying to save him from Voldemort.

Dumbledore's agents also provide help and guidance to Harry when Dumbledore cannot help. For example, Hagrid must physically bring Harry his admission letter from Hogwarts because Harry's uncle refuses to let Harry see the letter. Hagrid tells Harry that he is a wizard, introduces him to the wizarding world, and provides Harry with advice and friendship throughout the series. In book three, <u>Harry Potter and the Prisoner of Azkaban</u>, Professor Lupin teaches Harry the Patronus charm to help him defend himself against the Dementors. He also follows Harry and his friends and helps uncover the truth behind the betrayal of Harry's parents to Voldemort. In <u>The Chamber of Secrets</u>, Fawkes, Dumbledore's phoenix, aids Harry by bringing him the Sorting Hat from which Harry pulls the sword of Gryffindor to fight and kill the basilisk. Even Professor Snape helps Harry when he mutters the counter curse against Quirrell's attempt to make Harry fall from his broom during a Quidditch match in the first book. Professor Snape helps Harry at various times throughout the series and Harry finally comes to understand why Snape helped him but also disliked him.

On the journey the hero usually has companions. The companions serve a variety of functions. They may offer balance for the hero, they may help the hero in battle, or they may help the hero learn valuable lessons. Odysseus begins the journey back to Ithaca with his crew, but all are lost before the journey is completed.

Sam stays by Frodo's side throughout the quest and is a faithful and loyal companion. Sam, Merry, and Pippin also help Frodo on his quest. Frodo is reluctant to take anyone with him on his journey to Rivendell, but Sam reminds him that Gandalf told Frodo not to go alone, but to "take someone as [he] can trust" on the journey. (Tolkien "Fellowship" 118) In Rivendell, Aragorn, Boromir, Legolas, and Gimli pledge to help Frodo on his quest to Mount Doom.

Harry's friends Ron and Hermione help Harry in his quest. All three are in the House of Gryffindor, and together the three of them decipher riddles, fight foes, and help one another out of difficulties. Harry and Ron have some typical adolescent conflicts but the friendship is solid and Ron is there when Harry needs him. Hermione is the smart and clever member of the group. She spends a great deal of time in the library reading and knows many spells beyond her wizarding level. Professor Lupin tells Hermione, "You're the cleverest witch of your age I've ever met" (Rowling "Prisoner" 346). She is the group's conscious, she is a wealth of information for Harry, and it is she who usually comes up with the correct spell when they are in trouble.

The Hero's Trials and the Descent Into Darkness

Throughout the journey, the hero must face a series of challenges that are designed to test the hero. There are two types of challenges: physical and psychological. Physical challenges require the hero to perform courageous acts in battle, test the physical endurance of the hero, or require the hero to sacrifice some physical aspect of him or herself. Although physical challenges require strength, endurance, and skill, they often involve some psychological challenges as well. The hero must often figure out the best course of action or confront fears and insecurities in the process of completing the physical challenge. Psychological challenges appear at various times, even during sleep or resting. These are the inner trials and challenges the hero faces. The hero confronts fears, doubts, and insecurities about his or her character. Often, psychological challenges are as exhausting as physical challenges, and they require the hero to accept his or her limitations or character flaws.

The hero's journey or quest is always fraught with danger and the journey often requires the hero to descend into darkness. The darkness symbolizes "the unknown, and danger" (Campbell "Heroes" 77), and the darkness is a test of the hero's bravery and wit because in the darkness the hero cannot see his or her way. In literature, evil has always been associated with darkness, and in the dark, heroes must draw on all their courage to face what can and cannot be seen. The hero must delve into the unknown and this requires physical and psychological strength. Venturing into dark places is symbolic of the hero's descent into his or her own soul. In the darkness, the hero must face the unknown physical monster as well as the hero's own personal demons. Darkness is one of the journey's trials that test the hero, and only through these challenges can the hero discover previously unknown strengths. When the challenge is completed, the hero returns to the light which symbolizes the hero's growth and newfound knowledge.

Odysseus enters the cave of the Cyclops where he must outwit the creature in order to save himself and his men, and then use physical strength to blind the monster in order to escape. Later in The Odyssey, Odysseus must overcome fear and enter the underworld where no living person should enter. In the underworld, Odysseus meets people from his past, including Achilles and his mother, and he learns what has happened in Ithaca during his absence. This is a task that is physically and psychologically draining for Odysseus.

In the same tradition, both Frodo and Harry often descend into darkness. Frodo is given a phial containing "the Light of Earendil's star" (Tolkien "Fellowship" 423). The gift represents hope and courage because Earendil was a man who journeyed to see the Valar, the ruling powers of Middle Earth, to ask for their help in Middle Earth. The Valar granted his request and placed him as a constellation in the heavens to guide seamen at night and give them hope. The phial "bestows hope and courage" (Colbert 138) to Frodo when he most needs it. For example, when Frodo enters a dark cave in The Two Towers he soon finds a monster in the darkness. The cave is the lair of Shelob and Frodo must use the phial to repel the giant spider. Galadriel told Frodo it is "A light when all other lights go out!" (Tolkien "Towers" 372) and in the cave not only was it dark, but Frodo was afraid and losing hope. The light repelled the spider and gave Frodo hope and courage.

Harry Potter also descends into darkness numerous times and faces the unknown monster. In The Chamber of Secrets, Harry must descend into the chamber deep under the school to rescue Ginny. There he finds the giant basilisk and must battle it. In book six, <u>Harry Potter and the Half Blood Prince</u>, Harry and Dumbledore enter "what seemed total darkness" (Rowling 560) as they attempt to find one of Lord Voldemort's Horcruxes in a dark water-filled cave. Inside the cave, Harry encounters Inferi, an army of the dead, who attempt to drag him down into the water.

Perhaps the darkest place to which Harry descends is when he walks into the forest to face Voldemort in <u>Harry Potter and the Deathly Hallows</u>. As Harry walks to certain death, he is accompanied by his deceased loved ones via a magical stone and is able to accept his forthcoming death. However, when Voldemort attempts to kill him with the *Avada Kedavra* curse, Harry enters into a state of limbo because the two are bound to one another. Voldemort unknowingly made Harry a Horcrux when he attempted to kill him as a baby. As a result, a part of Voldemort lived inside Harry. Voldemort further strengthened the bond and the protection Harry's mother gave Harry when she died when Voldemort took Harry's blood to regenerate his body. Sitting with Dumbledore in limbo, Harry learns a great deal about himself, but he must make a decision: stay and go on, or return in the hopes of killing Voldemort.

The hero is not always the strongest individual in a story, but often the hero exhibits qualities other than strength such as cunning, guile, and mental fortitude. This is important because not all obstacles or challenges can be overcome by brute force. Attributes such as intelligence, kindness, and understanding are as important as strength and courage in the hero's journey. Odysseus uses "all his wiles and wits to get himself out of one fix after another" (65 Cahill) as he outwits the Cyclops and tricks Calypso. Once

Odysseus reaches the shores of Ithaca he must continue on alone because only he can reclaim his home and family.

Like all heroes, on his journey to destroy the Ring Frodo "discovers noble qualities he never imagined he had, such as bravery, strength, determination, and patience" (Colbert 13). The archetype of the hero is often the character that is not born great, but the person who is forced to become great. Physical strength is required to some degree, but it is mental agility that allows the hero to fulfill the quest.

Frodo must resist the power of the Ring and he is determined to get to Mount Doom and destroy it. Frodo knows the Ring is trying to return to Sauron and will corrupt anyone who touches it, so he decides to split from the others and head off alone. Alone in the forest, he says aloud to himself as if to convince himself that his action is right, "I will do now what I must...the evil of the Ring is already at work even in the Company, and the Ring must leave them before it does more harm. I will go alone." (Tolkien "Fellowship" 451) Frodo is afraid, but he summons the inner courage to break with the Fellowship and continue on alone, exhibiting strength he never knew he possessed.

Harry too exhibits great inner strength and wit. Like the hero Oedipus from the Greek tragedy Oedipus Rex, Harry must outwit the Sphinx during the third task of the Tri-Wizard Tournament to get to the center of the maze where, like Theseus, he encounters the hidden danger in the maze, in this case a port key that transports him to an encounter with Lord Voldemort. Like Frodo, Harry must summon inner courage when he realizes he must discover the truth about Lord Voldemort's horcruxes "before he could move a little farther along the dark and winding path stretching ahead of him...[a path] he now knew he would have to journey alone." (Rowling "Half Blood

Prince" 635-6) Harry is sad that he must venture on alone, but he is determined to complete his task.

The monsters and physical dangers the heroes of modern literature face are challenging and are often drawn from mythology. Odysseus must face several monsters in The Odyssey including a Cyclops. Theseus battles the deformed half-man half-bull Minotaur, and Hercules faces the Cerberus, the three-headed dog that guards the entrance to the underworld. In Greek mythology, centaurs are half-man half-horse creatures that represent chaos. Centaurs are depicted on the friezes of the Parthenon and are for the most part, "savage creatures, more like beasts than men." (Hamilton "Mythology" 48). However, one of the centaurs, Chiron, "was known everywhere for his goodness and his wisdom" (Hamilton "Mythology" 48). The hero Jason was raised by Chiron after his father King Aeson of Iolchos was defeated by his stepbrother and the king feared for his son's safety. Tolkien and Rowling draw on mythological monsters to create hideous and terrifying creatures to challenge their own heroes.

Although Frodo does not do much physical fighting on his journey he does face goblins, orcs, and Shelob the giant spider. Like many mythological creatures, these creatures are fearsome and grotesque. In Shelob's lair, the giant spider hunts Frodo and Frodo desperately tries to escape. In Moria, Frodo is speared by a cave troll and he encounters the Balrog of Morgoth, a creature "both a shadow and a flame, strong and terrible" (Tolkien "Fellowship" 399). However, it is the Ring Wraiths or Nazgul "nine beings, slaves of the Nine Rings and the chief servants of Sauron...[who] wielded a great power and terror" (Foster 358-9) that are the most frightening to Frodo. These creatures are neither living nor dead. They are the former kings of men who each were given a Ring so they could be enslaved by the One

Ring. They hunt Frodo and the Ring and it is the king of the Nazgul who stabs Frodo in the shoulder with a cursed blade on Weathertop and inflicts an injury that will haunt Frodo forever.

Harry Potter also must face a host of mythological creatures and monsters. Like Tolkien, Rowling created a giant spider, Aragog. Harry and Ron must venture into the dark Forbidden Forest and find Aragog to discover exactly what happened the first time the Chamber of Secrets was opened fifty years earlier. In the first book of the series, Harry faces Fluffy, the Cerberus that guards the trap door leading to the hiding place of the Sorcerer's Stone. Harry also has encounters with Centaurs, who true to the description of the mythological creatures cannot come to an agreement on whether to join the fight against Voldemort, join Voldemort against the wizards, or remain neutral. In The Sorcerer's Stone, Firenze is the good and wise centaur that, to the dismay of the other centaurs, saves Harry when Harry is in the forbidden forest. In Book five, Hagrid must step in and save Firenze or the other centaurs "would have kicked Firenze to death [because] they were angry that Firenze went to work for Dumbledore" (Rowling "Phoenix" 686). Firenze, who believes in negotiation, forgiveness, and good, parts with the centaurs and seeks refuge in Hogwarts. He is the centaur who stands on the side of good just as Chiron did in the ancient Greek myth.

Many of the epic heroes of mythology and literature fight the monsters they encounter on their journey with a sword. A sword is a talisman and usually has special significance to the hero and is a part of the hero's persona. Fighting with a sword takes courage and strength, and it brings the hero face to face with the enemy. Fighting with a sword is similar to hunting with a spear or sword, and as discussed earlier, some of the earliest myths involved hunting because of the dangers involved. The story of Odysseus is inspirational because Odysseus is one of the heroes of Troy who faced terrible odds and returned triumphant. The sword is an ancient weapon that symbolizes strength and greatness and is often handed down from one generation to the next. When Theseus travels to meet his father King Aegeus, he takes the sword left for him by his father so his father would recognize him. Sometimes heroes' swords are magical, such as King Arthur's sword Excalibur, which was an unbreakable sword made by an Avalonian elf.

Frodo inherits the magical sword Sting from Bilbo, a sword made by elves that glows blue when orcs are nearby. In Moria, Boromir's blade was notched trying to stab at an orc, yet when Frodo "stabbed with Sting at the hideous foot. There was a bellow, and the foot jerked back" (Tolkien "Fellowship" 364). Frodo's magical blade was able to penetrate what a regular blade could not.

Harry uses a ruby-encrusted silver sword that once belonged to Godric Gryffindor, one of the founders of Hogwarts and the original head of Gryffindor House of which Harry is a member. Dumbledore tells Harry, "only a true Gryffindor could have pulled that [sword] out of the hat" (Rowling "Chamber" 334). Harry pulled the Sword of Gryffindor out of the Sorting Hat and used it to kill the Basilisk down in the Chamber of Secrets.

The hero's journey is physical, but it is also psychological because the hero must battle his or her inner doubts and insecurities. In The Odyssey, Odysseus despairs many times that he will never reach his home, and he pleads with Poseidon to help him understand what is required of him. Eventually, Poseidon allows Odysseus to return home where he faces more challenges. Frodo too despairs that he will not be able to carry the Ring to Mordor. He tells Sam, "I can't manage it... it is such a weight to carry, such a weight" (Tolkien "King" 228). He confides to Sam that he cannot bear to carry the Ring anymore and, like Odysseus, Frodo fears that he will never see his home, the Shire, again because the weight of the Ring is becoming excruciating.

Harry also fears that he will not succeed. He is often upset that he must face Voldemort and some of the creatures that he must face, such as the Dementors, terrify him. When Harry tries to protect Sirius from the Dementors he too is attacked and Dementors begin to suck out his soul. "A paralyzing terror filled Harry" and in his mind he heard his mother scream and feared it "was going to be the last thing he ever heard" (Rowling "Prisoner" 384). In Harry Potter and the Deathly Hallows, Harry called the quest "a pointless and rambling journey", and he feared Ron and Hermione were "disappointed by his poor leadership" (Rowling "Hallows" 292).

The fear of failure is ever-present for the hero on the journey and is one of the many obstacles that the hero must overcome. He or she grows and matures because of the journey, and it is through the physical and psychological trials that the hero learns about himself or herself and about the world.

Homecoming

Once the hero faces the challenges and accomplishes the task then the hero must return home, but how the hero accomplishes the return varies with each myth and story. Sometimes, the hero must flee from pursuing forces, such as Jason did after having accomplished his goal of obtaining the Golden Fleece. Returning with the aid of supernatural help is another convention of the hero in mythology. Sometimes circumstances dictate that the hero is "brought back from his supernatural adventure by assistance from without... the world may have to come and get him" (Campbell "Hero" 207). Athene aided Odysseus when he returned home by turning him into an old man so he could covertly discover what was happening in Ithaca and formulate a plan to reclaim his home.

Frodo and Harry are heroes who are aided in their return home and rescued by the world they saved. At the end of Return of the King, Frodo destroys the Ring, but he and Sam are stranded on a large rock surrounded by lava that pours out of Mount Doom. Gandalf sends the mighty eagles to rescue Frodo and Sam and bring them safely back to Gondor, the home of the king.

At the end of each book, after completing a part of the overall journey, Harry must return to Hogwarts before he returns to his aunt and uncle's house. Sometimes, Harry receives supernatural help to get back to Hogwarts. For example, at the end of book two, Dumbledore's phoenix, Fawkes, carries Harry, Ron, Ginny, and Professor Lockhart out of the Chamber of Secrets far below Hogwarts. At the end of book four, a magical port key brings Harry back to Hogwarts after a near fatal encounter with a fully regenerated Lord Voldemort and his minions of Death Eaters. At other times a person rescues Harry as happened at the end of <u>Harry Potter and the Sorcerer's Stone</u> when Dumbledore finds him unconscious after his encounter with Lord Voldemort and brings him to the hospital wing.

Harry has a "homecoming" at the end of each school year that culminates with the seventh book. Each year, Harry returns to the Dursley's home for the summer and each year his experience at the house is different because Harry has changed as a result of events that took place during the previous school year. For example, at the end of book one, Harry realizes that the Dursleys, who are afraid of magic, will be afraid of him when he returns for the summer. He says, "They don't know we're not allowed to use magic at home. I'm going to have a lot of fun with Dudley this summer" (Rowling "Sorcerer" 309). When Harry returns to the Dursley's home they are afraid of him and try to forbid him to do magic. They are as unhappy to see Harry as he is to see them. However, Harry must return each year so that the protection his mother gave him when she died will remain intact. At the end of the sixth book Harry says, I'm going back to the Dursley's once more, because Dumbledore wanted me to...but it'll be a short visit, and then I'll be gone for good" (Rowling "Half Blood Prince" 650). Harry decides to leave the Dursley's home for good and he plans to return to Godric's Hollow because "it started there, all of it" (Rowling "Half Blood Prince" 631). That is the place where Harry had a home with his parents, where his parents died, and where he survived the Avada Kedavra killing curse. Therefore, in a sense, when Harry finally returns to Godric's Hollow he will be returning home for the first time. Harry will return to the place where it all began.

Heroes often must fight to regain their home and take their place in society. In their absence, home changes and often needs to be restored before the hero can finally rest. Odysseus must fight the suitors, who thinking Odysseus was dead, wished to marry his wife Penelope and gain control of Ithaca.

Frodo returns to the Shire and he, Sam, Merry, and Pippin must fight to take back control from those who have taken over. Sam tells Farmer Cotton, a Hobbit who has been waiting for a chance to get rid of the newcomers, that he, Frodo, and the others are "raising the Shire. We're going to clear out these ruffians, and their Chief too" (Tolkien "Return" 311). Saruman the wizard has taken up residence in the Shire and is behind the takeover, but after the battle to free the Shire, Frodo spares his life. However, Saruman provokes his minion Wormtongue who snaps and kills Saruman. This is the last battle to save Middle Earth.

The castle is also Harry's home and he dreads leaving it every year. Upon his return to Hogwarts in <u>Harry Potter and the Deathly Hallows</u>, Harry must fight to regain control of the castle from Voldemort and the Death Eaters. The castle is Harry's real home because it is the only true home he has ever known. It is the place he feels most comfortable, where he can be himself, and where he is the happiest. With his friends surrounding him in the Room of Requirement, Harry announced, "We're fighting" (Rowling "Hallows" 604), and the battle for Hogwarts began, a battle that would cost Harry dearly, but would finally see the end of Voldemort.

Once the hero makes it home that is not always the end of the story because now the hero must reintegrate into the community after the perilous adventure. The hero must "accept as real, after an experience of the soul-satisfying vision of fulfillment, the passing joys and sorrows, banalities and noisy obscenities of life." (Campbell "Hero" 218). Compared to the adventure, normal life can seem boring and the life the hero returns to is never the same as the one the hero left. After killing the suitors, Odysseus can rest and all were glad, but he still had to get reacquainted with his wife and his now grown child.

Frodo returns to the Shire after his adventure, but the Shire has changed and eventually he must leave. He says, "I have been too deeply hurt, Sam. I tried to save the Shire, and it was saved, but not for me" (Tolkien "King" 338). The quest to destroy the Ring took a toll on Frodo and he cannot stay in the world. Like other heroes who "have taken up residence forever in the blessed isle of the unaging Goddess of Immortal Being" (Campbell "Heroes" 193), Frodo sails off on the elven ship to take refuge in the mystical realm of Valinor where he can be at peace.

Like Odysseus and Frodo, at the end of the adventure, Harry too wants nothing more than to rest. He tells Ron and Hermione, "I've had enough trouble for a lifetime" (Rowling "Hallows" 749) as he heads off to his bed in Griffindor tower after defeating Voldemort. Harry wants to live a quiet life and die a natural death because he is now the owner of the Elder Wand. The wand is the most powerful of all wizard wands and wizards have killed to possess it. The wand must be won in battle and Harry wisely concludes if he dies "a natural death…its power will be broken" (Rowling "Hallows" 749) and fighting for possession of the wand will end.

During the course of the journey the hero grows and comes of age because he or she moves from naiveté to knowledge. The hero returns home older, wiser, and stronger because of the challenges that were faced along the way. Frodo's journey took about a year, and when he returns to the Shire he is no longer the scared Hobbit he was when he left. He has faced death numerous times and he has survived. Harry grows up with every book and he too discovers talents and strengths that he never knew he possessed. Yes, Frodo and Harry have flaws; they have fears, self-doubt, and they make the wrong decisions at times. However, essentially they are both good people who try to do what is best not for their own self interest, but best for society. Therefore, they are both role models for readers and they illuminate the human condition.

Epic Hero Adventure Stories

Long ago Homer established the hero and journey archetype, yet it is still used today by authors who wish to create epic hero adventure stories. The reader sees greater meaning in the story when the reader understands that the story comes from a long tradition and illustrates part of the human condition. Scholars, such as Joseph Campbell and Anne Petty agree. Understanding the foundation of modern works of literature and the mythology behind such works gives the reader a greater understanding of what it is to be human, the human condition. The universal themes upon which mythology and modern literature are built are the "basic elements of humanity... the struggle to survive, the need to interact with others of our kind, and the search for meaning within that interaction" are constants regardless of the century (Petty 14). Literature illustrates the human condition because it shows the reader what it is to be human with all the frailties and all the strengths of humanity.

There has always been a need for heroes in humans' lives. We all recognize that we are part of a larger society and "the hero is the one who has given his physical life to some order of realization of that truth" (Campbell "Power of Myth" 138). Every individual must face the challenges of life and literature shows the reader how to face those challenges and triumph.

Mythology teaches people about the human condition and about the universal values of good and evil. Joseph Campbell states, "the ultimate aim of the hero's quest must be neither release nor ecstasy for oneself, but the wisdom and power to serve others" (Campbell "Power of Myth" xiv). Odysseus learns piety and reverence on his journey. While he is away, his son grows up and Odysseus misses it. Frodo's journey is a selfless act to save Middle Earth and ensure the time of men. He gives up everything for the quest and must leave the Shire because of his injuries. Harry's journey is to pick up the task begun by his parents to save the world from Lord Voldemort who is bent on destroying it. Harry succeeds, but it costs the lives of many of his friends and he is forever changed. Frodo, Harry, and other epic heroes put society and community ahead of personal needs, desires, and ambitions. Despite the danger, they accept the call to adventure and they act without regard for their personal safety because they are individuals with high morals and character. Heroes show the reader the depth of human endurance, perseverance, and fortitude.

CHAPTER IV

CONCLUSION

The Relevance of Mythology

"The Lord of the Rings" and "Harry Potter" are two cultural icons of literature by which classical mythology is transmitted to a modern audience. Through the use of the literary archetypes of the hero and the journey, new generations of readers are not only entertained, but they are educated in the ways of the world. Frodo and Harry are exemplary heroes because, despite their flaws, they strive to do what is right. They face terrible odds, fierce creatures, and evil, yet they triumph over adversity and discover physical and psychological strength they never imagined they possessed. Although the situations Frodo and Harry face are extraordinary, by reading about the struggles of the two protagonists, modern readers can identify with the struggles each hero faces and acquire insight to overcoming personal struggles in life.

Mythology and literature that includes mythology are instructive and timeless because they help a person navigate through the obstacles of life and provide guides for living. The struggles of the protagonists in literature and the heroes of mythology provide examples of how to deal with problems in our own lives and help the reader to recognize solutions and truths about the human condition. The reader identifies with the struggling hero and "suffers with the hero [through] his trials and tribulations, and triumphs with him as virtue is victorious...and the inner and outer struggles of the hero imprint morality" on the reader. (Bettelheim "Enchantment" 9) The reader may be struggling through trials different from those of the hero, but the success of the hero over adversity assures the reader that there is hope for him or her as well.

Readers of all ages but children particularly benefit from coming of age stories because they provide examples of individuals who struggle and overcome adversity. In "The Lord of the Rings", Frodo finds within himself the strength to carry the Ring of power to Mount Doom. Through the trials he must face and the obstacles he must overcome to achieve his task, Frodo comes of age. He discovers inner strengths and courage and physical strength that he never believed he possessed. Harry Potter is also coming of age through the course of the series of seven books because the process of maturation is central to the plot. Like Frodo, Harry faces trials and challenges through which he realizes his inner strength and fortitude, but Harry also is physically and emotionally growing up with every book, and he faces the everyday trials and challenges that all adolescents face as they grow up.

Literature can be read on two levels: the surface level that reveals the action and events of the story, and the deeper level that reveals something about the human condition. Within the deeper meaning of the story is the universal truth that the author wishes to convey to the reader. Reading mythology is important to understanding literature because "literature develops out of, or is preceded by, a body of myths, legends, folktales, which are transmitted by our earlier classics [and] to grow up in ignorance of what is in the Bible or Homer is as crippling to the imagination as being deprived of the multiplication table" (Frye "Learning" 44). Therefore, understanding mythology helps the reader identify the deeper meaning of the story because many authors use mythological references to transmit universal messages to the reader.

Throughout the various stages of life, myth and ritual guide individuals by providing insight into problems and sometimes proposing solutions. Myths help the adult throughout life by providing insight into marriage, parenthood, relationships, and death. Through mythology, the individual receives information regarding "the themes that have supported human life, built civilizations, and informed religions over the millennia" (Campbell "Power of Myth" 2). Rituals derived from myths are essentially, "emotional and social 'fences' and templates. They provide people with behavior boundaries, procedures for solving problems, prompts for acting appropriately, patterns for celebrations, and ways for coping with the emotions and social implications attending life's landmark events, such as losing loved ones (funerals) and creating the next generation of families (weddings)" (Greenberg).Therefore, myths are important models of behavior that help a person through life's turning points and obstacles, and the rituals associated with myths bind people together and provide a sense of belonging to a community.

Rituals associated with coming of age are important because they provide milestones or markers that let children know they are advancing toward adulthood. Myths are "derived from, or give symbolic expression to, initiation rites or other *rites of passage*" (Bettelheim "Enchantment" 35). All cultures and religions have coming of age rituals that signal when a child is no longer a child but a recognized adult member of the community. For example, in Athens in the 4th century B.C., eighteen-year old boys "went to a temple and swore obedience to the constitution" (Hamilton "Echo of

Greece" 52). Swearing an oath signaled the youth's entrance into adulthood and the beginning of his obligation to the polis. In the Catholic religion when a young person makes the sacrament of Confirmation he or she is recognized as an adult member of the church. The Bat Mitzvah for girls and the Bar Mitzvah for boys are the ceremonies by which a young Jewish girl or boy becomes recognized as an adult in the Jewish community. Prior to becoming an adult member of any community, the youth receives instruction in the laws, expected behavior, and obligations to the community. Often an adult member of the community testifies that the youth is prepared to undertake the obligations of adulthood. All children look for ways to validate their entry into adulthood, and rituals help children recognize the milestone of coming of age.

Coming of age stories provide a model for the transition into adulthood. The hero and the journey archetypes are often incorporated into coming of age stories because in order to grow and mature, both physically and emotionally, we all must struggle with obstacles such as indecision, insecurity, and fear. The struggles of the protagonists in literature are often drawn from mythology and provide examples of how to deal with problems in our own lives. Those members of the audience who are able to recognize the mythology gain a greater understanding of the stories. Incorporating mythology helps the author get to the heart of humanity, and mythology's inclusion provides a bridge to the past. Therefore, in order to fully understand and appreciate literature, a person must have a basic understanding of ancient mythology and of the "old stories" including folklore, fairy tales, and fables.

Mythology is an important part of many works of modern literature, and since Western society has its foundation in ancient Greece and Rome it is therefore important for people to learn about these two ancient cultures. Democracy, literature, art, and architecture all incorporate the ideas first established in Greece in the 6th century B.C. Understanding the past is important because it tells us from where we come. Mythology is relevant to the modern person because it provides a guide to life and the many lessons of mythology are applicable to modern life.

Beyond The Lord of the Rings and Harry Potter

"Things are not untrue just because they never happened. In people's minds they are far more real." (Hamley 88)

Reading the "old stories" teaches children about the past, and it is an important component in the development of children's imaginations. Children need to read mythology because mythology guides them through the stages of life and because these "old stories" tell children about the culture from which they are descended. At its website, The Library Foundation promotes a variety of programs for children to encourage reading because "as children read, they practice empathetic imagination, prediction, and other higher level critical thinking skills. Most importantly, they gain experience picturing new possibilities and dreaming about a better future" (1). Reading stories, including fantasy stories, provides a safe environment for children to try out new situations and possibilities.

Fantasy stories are often deemed escapist stories, but they are complex stories with fully developed characters, intricate plots, and descriptive language. Fantasy stories confront unpleasant aspects of life such as injustice, cruelty, rejection, and death, and the stories propose solutions to those unpleasantries. Unlike realistic stories that may not end happily, fantasy stories generally end on a hopeful note and "without fantasies to give us hope, we do not have the strength to meet the adversities of life" (Bettelheim "Enchantment" 121). Through fantasy novels, children are able to leave the confines of the real world and experience the adversities of life in a vicarious manner and see that there is hope no matter how terrible the adversity.

Many critics of fantasy novels claim that fantasy stories are unreal and they distract readers from the reality of life. Tom Shipley, who knew and taught with Tolkien at Oxford, argues that fantasy literature and Tolkien's works in particular are not escapist literature. In an interview with CNN correspondent Jamie Allen, Shipley says, "The Lord of the Rings is actually all about what happened in the 20th century." Far from being escapist, the novels are about "more than the adventures of hobbits and elves and wizards and other creatures who delve into a war over ultimate power in Middle Earth...they are a reflection of the 20th century's turbulent history" (Allen). The story reflects the realities of life because beneath the surface story of elves and men fighting orcs and goblins for control of Middle Earth is one of the realities of life. War!

The inclusion of magic in fantasy stories often draws the largest criticism, especially from parents who worry that the use of magic will lure children and young adults away from good and towards evil. "The Lord of the Rings" has been challenged because of the use of magic, but the "Harry Potter" series has faced broader criticism and has been on the most challenged books list of the American Library Association since the first book in the series was published. What some people who are unfamiliar with the genre of fantasy fail to realize is that beneath the imaginative worlds, the bizarre creatures, and the magic, fantasy, like all literature, is about life and the human condition.

The characters of fantasy stories may or may not be human, yet they exhibit human characteristics as they struggle with acceptance, relationships, and internal and external challenges. The hero is often an unlikely hero because he or she may be flawed, as are many of the heroes of the "old stories". The hero may believe himself or herself to be unworthy in some way or to be incapable of accomplishing the task because the character's true talent has yet to be realized. Following the hero on a quest teaches the reader about human frailty, compassion, perseverance, and hope because eventually the hero does realize his or her potential and is successful in the quest.

Reading and making up stories is an activity that expands children's imaginations and allows them to experience something that would not be possible in the real world. Northrop Frye states, "one essential aspect of literacy training, and one that is possible to acquire, or begin acquiring, in childhood, is the art of listening to stories... it is what the army would call a basic training for the imagination" ("Learning" 43). Role-playing games and fan fiction are two avenues by which children can use their imagination to create their own stories based on characters from the books they know and love.

"The Lord of the Rings" and "Harry Potter" are series that help foster children's imaginations because they are intricate stories rich in mythology, but they are also valuable stories because reading the books provides a catalyst for conversation between children and adults. Harry Potter dominated the "NY Times bestseller list" for two years before a separate children's bestseller list was established in 2001, indicating readers were made up of more than children. University librarians and children's literature experts agree, "the Harry Potter series has inspired a new level of reading and conversation between both children and adults". (UNT News) "The Lord of the Rings" was voted the number one book of the 20th century in an Amazon.com poll and is now considered a "classic," showing it too has appeal to children and adults. "The Lord of the Rings", "Harry Potter", and "the fantasy genre, in particular, has found cross-generational success" (Lindrea) and has brought people of all ages together to discuss the books and movies.

The success of these novels has generated an explosion of new fantasy series and renewed interest in older fantasy series. New novels such as Eragon and Dragon Rider and older series such as Anne McCaffrey's many novels about Pern, a far off world colonized by humans, are stories involving heroes, dragons, and foreign lands that are exciting, imaginative and uplifting. J.R.R. Tolkien said fantasy does not deny sorrow, failure, and death because the possibility of these outcomes is necessary to feeling joy. What fantasy denies is "universal final defeat [thus] giving a fleeting glimpse of Joy" (Tolkien "Tree" 68). Through its heroes, fantasy novels empower readers because fantasy stories offer hope, solutions, and they show the reader what it is to be human.

END NOTES

[i] Vialou, Denis. Prehistoric Art and Civilization. Harry N. Abrams, Inc. New York: 1996.

[ii] Hamilton, Edith. Mythology. Boston: Little, Brown and Company, 1943.
Lister, Robin (retold). The Odyssey. Boston: King Fisher, 1987.
D'Aulaire, Ingri, Edgar Parin D'Aulaire. D'Aulaires' Book of Greek Myths. New York: Bantam Doubleday, 1962.

[iii] Campbell, Joseph. Myths to Live By. New York: Penguin Compass, 1972.
Campbell, Joseph. The Hero with a Thousand Faces. 3rd Ed. New Jersey: Princeton University Press, 1973.
Campbell, Joseph. The Power of Myth. New York: Anchor-Random House, 1988.

[iv] Petty, Anne. Tolkien in the Land of Heroes Discovery the Human Spirit. New York: Cold Springs Press, 2003.

[v] Tolkien Studies is an annual journal of Tolkien scholarship put out by West Virginia University and the West Virginia University Press. http://www.wvupress.com/journals/details.php?id=3

[vi] See John C. Hunter's article "The Evidence of Things Unseen: Critical Mythology and The Lord of the Rings" in the Winter 2006 edition of the Journal of Modern Literature that focuses on the mythic elements of the books in the context of post-war Western culture.

[vii] See Sharon Black's article "The Magic of Harry Potter: Symbols and Heroes of Fantasy" in the September 2003 edition of the Children's Literature in Education Journal that focuses on the reasons why two very different girls, a ten year old and a college student both like Harry Potter.

[viii] Dickerson, Matthew T., David L. O'Hara. From Homer to Harry Potter. Michigan: Brazos Press, 2006.

[ix] Baehr, Ted, Tom Snyder. Frodo and Harry – Understanding Visual Media and its Impact on our Lives. Illinois: Crossway Books, 2003.

[x] Colbert, David. The Magical Worlds of the Lord of the Rings. New York: Berkley Books Penguin, 2002.
Colbert, David. The Magical Worlds of Harry Potter. New York: Berkley Books Penguin, 2004

[xi] At the time of this writing because of the popularity of The Lord of the Rings and Harry Potter there are several conferences that discuss the books and movies. For example, each year the group Phoenix Rising hosts an interdisciplinary Harry Potter themed symposium and there are Tolkien conferences that examine all aspects of Tolkien's work.

[xii] There are many variations of the Creation myth. The myth presented in this chapter was compiled from the following sources: Hamilton, Edith. Mythology. Little, Brown and Company. Boston: 1942. Randall, Ronne. Myths and Legends. Barnes & Noble New York: 2001.

[xiii]The myth of Demeter and Persephone presented in this chapter was compiled from the following sources: Hamilton, Edith. Mythology. Little, Brown and Company. Boston: 1942. Randall, Ronne. Myths and Legends. Barnes & Noble New York: 2001.

[xiv] This myth of Aeneas was compiled from a variety of sources including a vase currently on display at the Boston Museum of Fine Art. Other sources include: Hamilton, Edith. Mythology. Little, Brown and Company. Boston: 1942. Randall, Ronne. Myths and Legends. Barnes & Noble New York: 2001.

WORKS CITED

Adams, Rebecca. "Bedtime rituals can help get kids tucked in." USA Today 24 April 2006. 24 January 2007 http://www.usatoday.com/news/health/2006-04-24-children-and-sleep_x.htm

Aeschylus. Oresteia. Trans. Richmond Lattimore. Chicago: University of Chicago Press, 1953.

Allen, Jamie. "The Secret of Tolkien's 'Rings". CNN 18 December 2001. 19 February 2007 http://archives.cnn.com/2001/SHOWBIZ/books/12/17/rings.tolkien/

Amarelo, Monica. "Neanderthals – First to Bury their Dead?" The American Association for the Advancement of Science 15 October 2002. 23 September 2006 http://www.aaas.org/news/releases/2002/1015dosers.shtml

Aristotle. Poetics. Trans. Malcolm Heath. New York: Penguin Classics, 1996.

Beowulf. Trans. Burton Raffel. New York: Penguin Signet Classic, 1963.

Bettelheim, Bruno. The Uses of Enchantment. New York: Alfred A. Knopf, Inc, 1976.

Boren, Henry C. Roman Society. 2nd ed. Lexington, MA: DC Heath & Company, 1992.

Bradford, Ernle. Thermopylae. Cambridge, MA: Da Capo Press, 1980.

Cahill, Thomas. Sailing the Wine Dark Sea Why the Greeks Matter. The Hinges of History. Vol. IV. New York: Doubleday, 2003.

Campbell, Joseph. Myths to Live By. New York: Penguin Compass, 1972.

Campbell, Joseph. The Hero with a Thousand Faces. 3rd Ed. New Jersey: Princeton University Press, 1973.

Campbell, Joseph. The Power of Myth. New York: Anchor-Random House, 1988.

Colbert, David. The Magical Worlds of the Lord of the Rings. New York: Berkley Books Penguin, 2002.

Coolidge, Olivia. Greek Myths. 1949. Boston: Houghton Mifflin Co., 1977.

Copleston, Frederick. The History of Philosophy. New York: Image Books. Doubleday, 1985.

Foster, Robert. Tolkien's World From A to Z The Complete Guide to Middle Earth. New York: Ballantine, 1978.

Frye, Northrop, Jay Macpherson. Biblical and Classical Myths: the mythological framework of Western Culture. Toronto: Macmillan, 1962.

Frye, Northrop. "The Developing Imagination." Learning in Language and Literature. Cambridge, MA: Harvard University Press, 1963.

Frye, Northrop. "Scholarship in a Post Literate World." Myth and Metaphor, Selected Essays. Ed. Robert D. Denham. Charlottesville: University of Virginia, 1990.

Greenberg, Polly. "Why Children Need Rituals and Routines, How our everyday rituals help children feel secure and ready to learn." Parents Magazine Sept 2000. 1 January 2007 http://ww2.sjc.edu/syc/article01.htm

Hamilton, Edith. Mythology. Boston: Little, Brown and Company, 1943.

Hamilton, Edith. The Echo of Greece. New York: WW Norton & Company, 1957.

Hamley, Dennis. Hare's Choice. Reprint Ed. New York: Yearling, 1992.

Hanson, Victor Davis. "No Glory that was Greece" What if? The World's foremost military historians imagine what might have been. Ed. Robert Cowley. New York: Penguin Putnam, 1999.

Harmon, William, Hugh Holman. A Handbook to Literature. 9th Ed. New Jersey: Prentice Hall, 2003.

Headden, Susan. "The Gift That was Greece." The Ancient World. U.S. News and World Report. Special Edition, 2004.

Homer. The Iliad. Trans. Richard Lattimore. Chicago: University of Chicago Press, 1951.

Janson, H.W., Anthony R. Janson. A Basic History of Art. New Jersey: Prentice Hall, 2003.

Kleiner, Fred S. Christin J. Mamiya. Gardner's Art through the ages, Western perspective. Volume I. 12th ed. California: Thomson Higher Education, 2006.

Lefkowitz, Mary. Greek Gods, Human Lives, What We Can Learn from Myths. New Haven: Yale University Press, 2003.

Lindrea, Victoria. "How Tolkien Triumphed Over the Critics" BBC News. 29 July 2004. 2 February 2007 http://news.bbc.co.uk/2/hi/entertainment/3935561.stm

Marten, Thomas R. Ancient Greece, From Prehistoric to Hellenistic Time. New Haven: Yale University Press, 2000.

The Library Foundation. Priorities. Early Literacy Programs. 26 January 2007 http://www.libraryfoundation.org/priorities/priorities_programs_print.html

Ner Le-Elef. Book of Quotations. 03 Feb 2004. 12 November 2006 www.nerleelef.com/Quotes.pdf.

Petty, Anne. Tolkien in the Land of Heroes Discovery the Human Spirit. New York: Cold Springs Press, 2003.

Pollitt, J.J. Art and Experience in Classical Greece. Cambridge: Cambridge University Press, 1972.

Randall, Ronne. The Children's Book of Myths and Legends. New York: Barnes & Noble, 2001.

Rowling, J.K. Harry Potter and the Chamber of Secrets. New York: Scholastic, 1999.

Rowling, J.K. Harry Potter and the Deathly Hallows. New York: Scholastic, 2007.

Rowling, J.K. Harry Potter and the Goblet of Fire. New York: Scholastic, 2000.

Rowling, J.K. Harry Potter and the Half-Blood Prince. New York: Scholastic, 2005.

Rowling, J.K. Harry Potter and the Order of the Phoenix. New York: Scholastic, 2003.

Rowling, J.K. Harry Potter and the Prisoner of Azkaban. New York: Scholastic, 1999.

Rowling, J.K. Harry Potter and the Sorcerer's Stone. New York: Scholastic, 1999.

Sophocles. Oedipus the King. Trans. H.D.F. Kitto. Oxford: Oxford University Press, 1994.

Strauss, Barry. The Battle of Salamis the Naval Encounter that Saved Greece – and Western Civilization. New York: Simon & Schuster, 2004.

Thiroux, Jacques. Krasemann, Keith. Ethics Theory and Practice. 10th Edition. New Jersey: Prentice Hall, 2009.

Tolkien, J.R.R. The Fellowship of the Ring. New York: Ballantine, 1973.

Tolkien, J.R.R. The Return of the King. New York: Ballantine, 1973.

Tolkien, J.R.R. The Silmarillion. New York: Ballantine, 1977.

Tolkien, J.R.R. Tree and Leaf. New Ed. New York: Harper Collins, 2001.

Tolkien, J.R.R. The Two Towers. New York: Ballantine, 1973.

Thucydides. History of the Peloponnesian War. Trans. Rex Warner. New York: Penguin Classics, 1972.

University of Maine Cooperative Extension. How Television Viewing Affects Children. 2006.   26   January   1007 http://www.umext.maine.edu/onlinepubs/htmpubs/4100.htm

University of North Texas News Service. Professor says Harry Potter Books Inspire Reading, Discussion Between Children and Adults. 18 June 2003. 2 February 2007. http://web2.unt.edu/news/story.cfm?story=8633

Made in the USA
Middletown, DE
12 January 2018